Published by The A320 Study Guide

Printed in Great Britain

Although every precaution has been taken in the preparation of this book, the publisher and author assume no responsibility for errors or omissions. Neither is any liability assumed for damages resulting from the use of information contained herein. All Technical details and procedures should be referenced to your own company manuals and these should be used as your primary reference.

ISBN 9798376980774

INTRODUCTION

Welcome to The A320 study guide. This has been written by pilots, for pilots. It is a guide to help maintain your knowledge of the A320 systems as well as certain procedures, and to give some tips on some of the more common failures that you may see in a simulator check.

All information has been collated from various sources and documents - with this in mind, please do not substitute this for your own company manuals, they remain your primary source of information. This guide however has been created to bring you all the pertinent information you need in one easy document. It covers only the essential knowledge required for day to day operations and to help with simulator assessments or command upgrade courses and preparation.

There are many variations between the A320 family and engine options for your airline so please check all information specific to your operation.

We hope you find this useful!

CONTENTS

- General Limitations 8
- Air Conditioning / Ventilation / Pressurisation 19
- Electrical 41
- Fire Protection 57
- Flight Controls 63
- Fuel 95
- Hydraulics 107
- Ice & Rain 121
- Landing Gear 127
- Lights 141
- Navigation 147
- Oxygen 159
- Pneumatic 167
- APU 171
- Powerplant 177

- Winter Operations 199
- Failure Management 209
- ECAM Warnings / Cautions 213
- Memory Items 215
- Performance 223
- CEO / NEO Differences 235
- Auto Flap Retract 237
- Tropopause and Atmosphere 239
- Performance / Idle Factor 243
- Navigation Accuracy 245
- Efficient Flying 249
- Performance Based Navigation 255

Procedures

- Standard Takeoff Technique 259
- Auto Flap Retract / Alpha Lock 260
- Rejected Takeoff 261
- Emergency Evacuation 262
- Climb 263
- Cruise 264
- Descent Preparation 267
- Descent 273
- Approach 277
- ILS Approach 284
- RNAV Approach 289
- Circling Approach 291
- Visual Approach 292
- Go Around / Baulked Landing 293
- Windshear 294
- PFD / ND Indications 297
- Flight Mode Annunciator Modes 305

A320neo

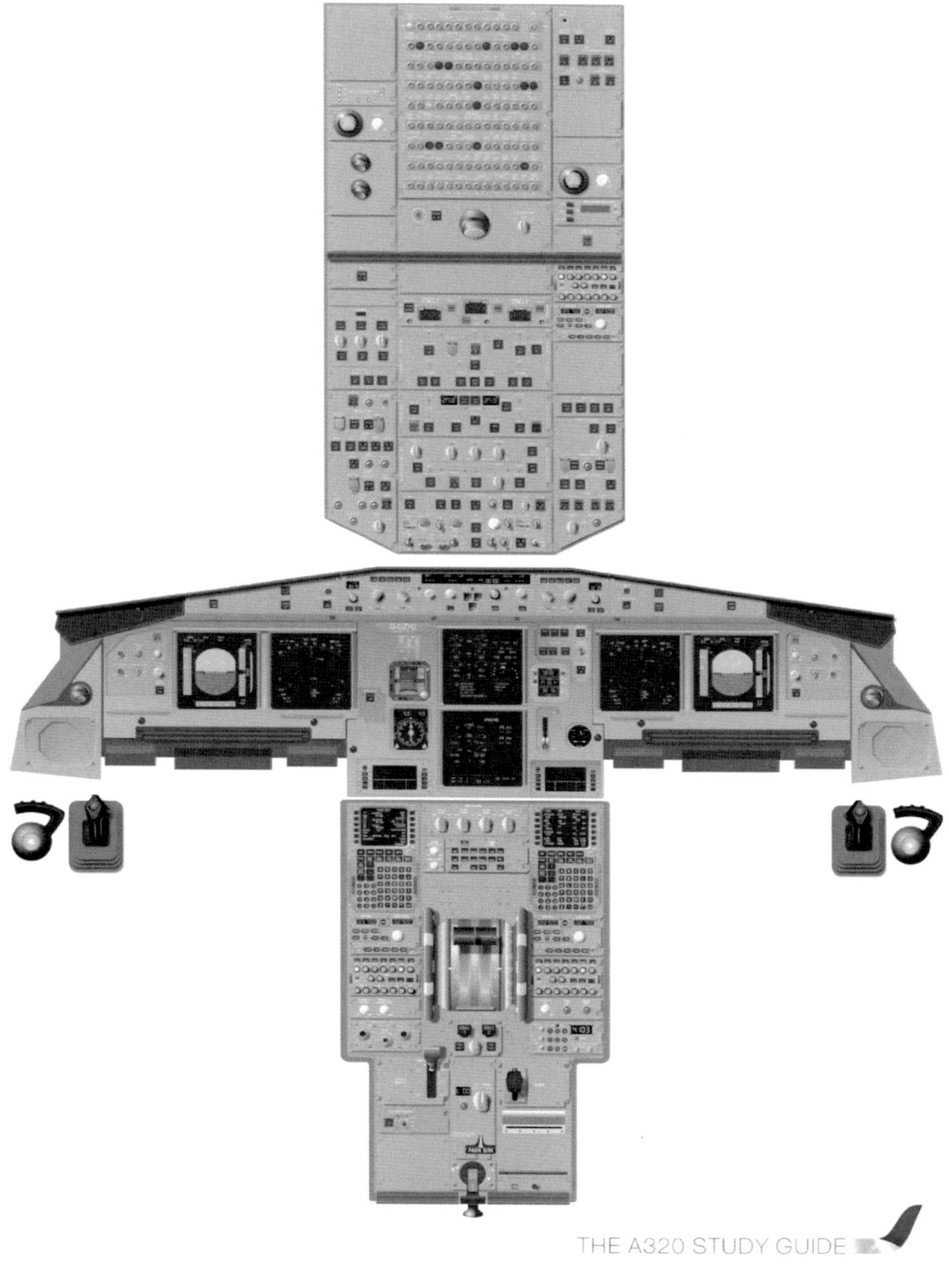

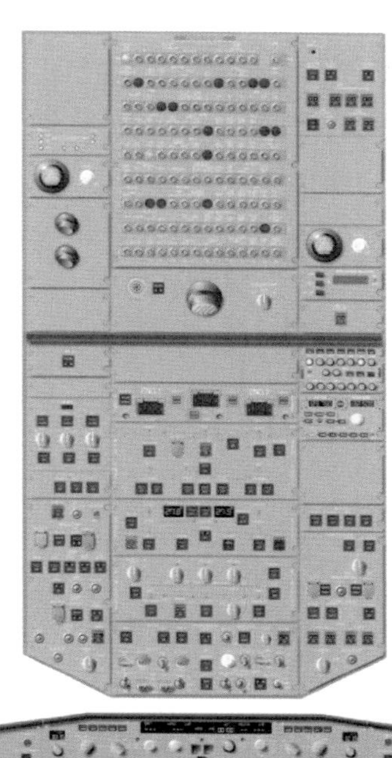

GENERAL LIMITATIONS

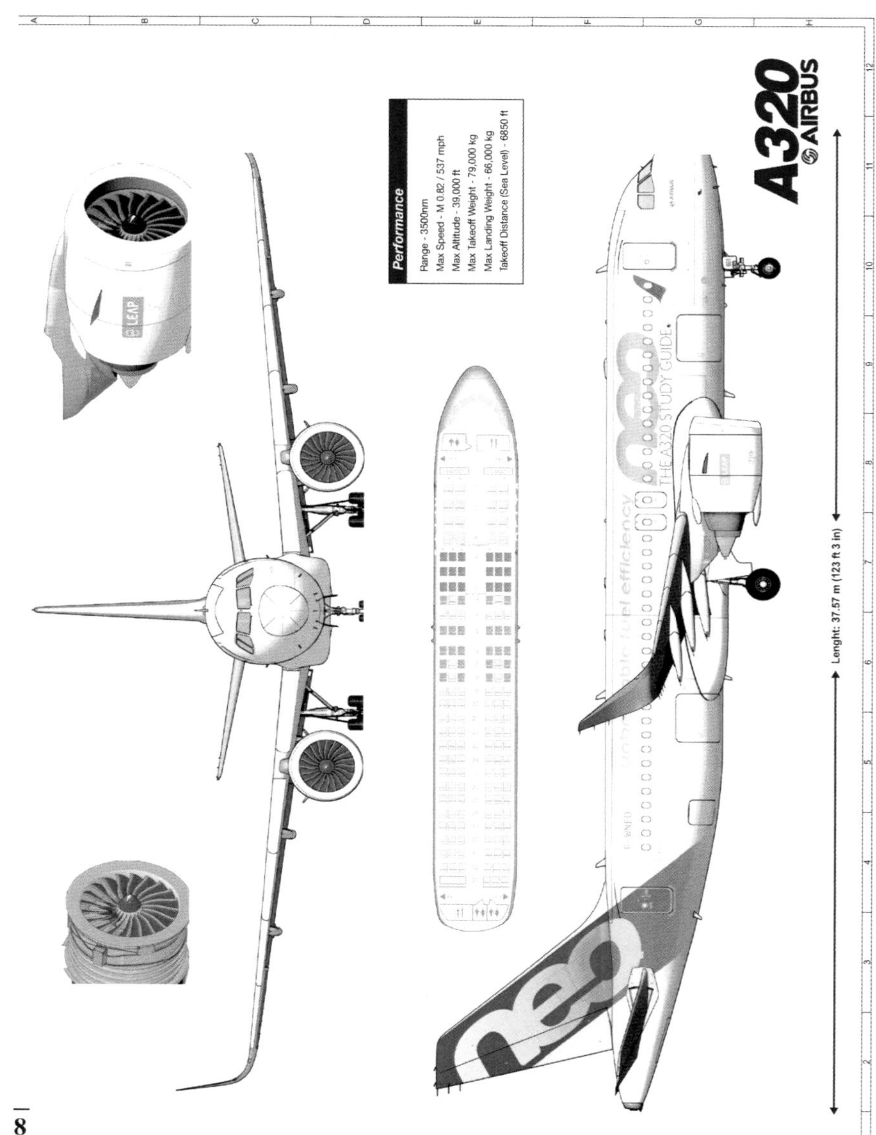

Aircraft Environmental Envelope

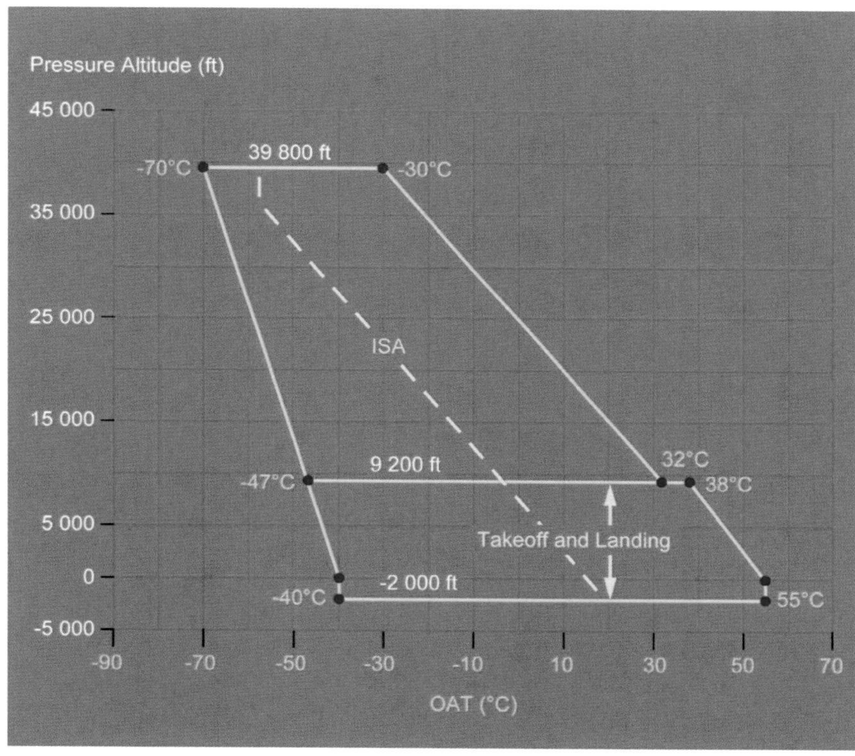

Maneuvering Load Limitations	
Clean Configurations	-1 g to +2.5 g
Other Configurations	0 g to +2 g

Wake Turbulence			
Departure	A380	3 Minutes	4 mins if intermediate
	Heavy	2 Minutes	3 mins if intermediate
Arrival	A380	7 nm	
	Heavy	5 nm	
	Other	3 nm	

Wind Limits		
	A319 / A320 CEO	**A320 / A321 NEO**
Passenger Door Operation	65 kts	65 kts
Cargo Door Operation	40 kts	40 kts
Max Crosswind Takeoff	38 kts (including Gust)	35 kts (including Gust)
Max Crosswind Landing	38 kts (including Gust)	38 kts (including Gust)
Tailwind Takeoff	15 kts	15 kts
Tailwind Landing	15 kts	15 kts

A319/A320 CEO Use Flap Full ONLY for tailwind greater than10 kts
A320 / A321 NEO Flap Full recommended for tailwind greater than 10 kts

Airport Limits	
Runway Slope	+/- 2%
Max Runway Altitude	14,100 ft
Standard Runway Width	45 m
Minimum Runway Width	30 m

Aircraft Max Operating Speeds	
Max Speed Cockpit Window Open	200 kts
VMO (Max Operating Speed)	350 kts
MMO (Max Mach)	M 0.82

Max Flap / Slat Speeds - A319 / A320			
Lever Position	Display Position	Max Speed	Phase
0		VMO/MMO	Cruise
1	1	230 kts	Holding
	1 + F	215 kts	Takeoff
2	2	200 kts	Takeoff / Approach
3	3	185 kts	Takeoff / App / Landing
FULL	FULL	177 kts	Landing

Max Flap / Slat Speeds - A321 NEO			
Lever Position	Display Position	Max Speed	Phase
0		VMO/MMO	Cruise
1	1	243 kts	Holding
	1 + F	225 kts	Takeoff
2	2	215 kts	Takeoff / Approach
3	3	195 kts	Takeoff / App / Landing
FULL	FULL	186 kts	Landing

Max Speeds - Landing Gear	
Max Speed Gear Extended - VLE	280 kts / M 0.67
Max Speed Gear Extension - VLO	250 kts / M 0.60
Max Speed Gear Retraction - VLO	220 kts / M 0.54
Max Tyre Speed	195 kts

Cockpit Wipers Speed	
Max Operational Speed	230 kts

Cabin Pressure Limitations	
Max Positive Differential Pressure	9.0 PSI
Max Negative Differential Pressure	-1.0 PSI
Safety Valve Operation	8.6 PSI

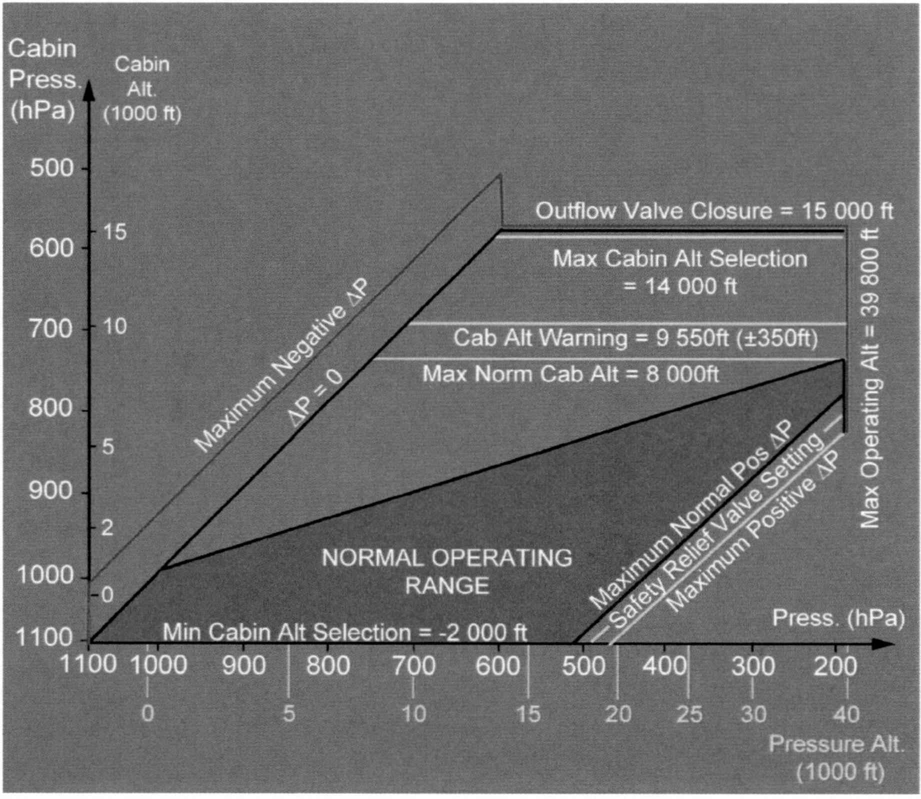

Autopilot Limitations	
Min Autopilot Engagement	100 ft / 5 seconds after takeoff
Approach G/S Mode	200 ft
Approach FINAL APP / V/S / FPA	250 ft
Circling Approach	500 ft
Cat 1 Displayed on FMA	160 ft
CAT2 / CAT3 Displayed on FMA	0 ft if Autoland Planned
PAR Approach	250 ft
Following Manual Go-Around	100 ft
CAT II ILS Min Decision	100 ft
CAT III A Min Decision	50 ft
CAT III B Min Decision	20 ft

Turbulence Penetration Speed		
A320 CEO	Below FL 200	250 kts
	Above FL 200	275 kts
	Above FL 300	M 0.76
A320 NEO	Below FL 200	260 kts
	Above FL 200	280 kts
	Above FL 300	M 0.76
A321 NEO	Below FL 200	275 kts
	Above FL 200	305 kts
	Above FL 300	M 0.76

APU Limitations	
APU Start	3 Consecutive start attempts, then wait 60 mins.
Max N Rotor Speed	107 %
Max EGT start below 35,000 ft	1090 °C
Max EGT start above 35,000 ft	1120 °C
Max EGT APU Running	675 °C

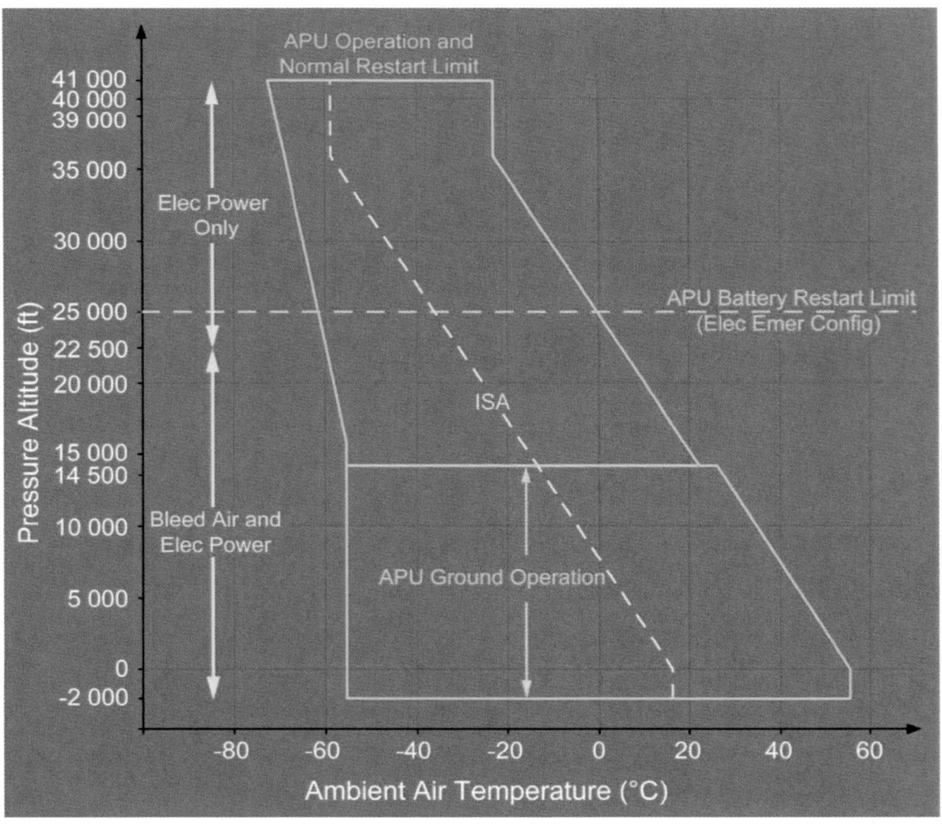

5.87 m
(19.26 ft)
4.14 m
(13.58 ft)
12.64 m
(41.47 ft)
5.07 m
(16.63 ft)

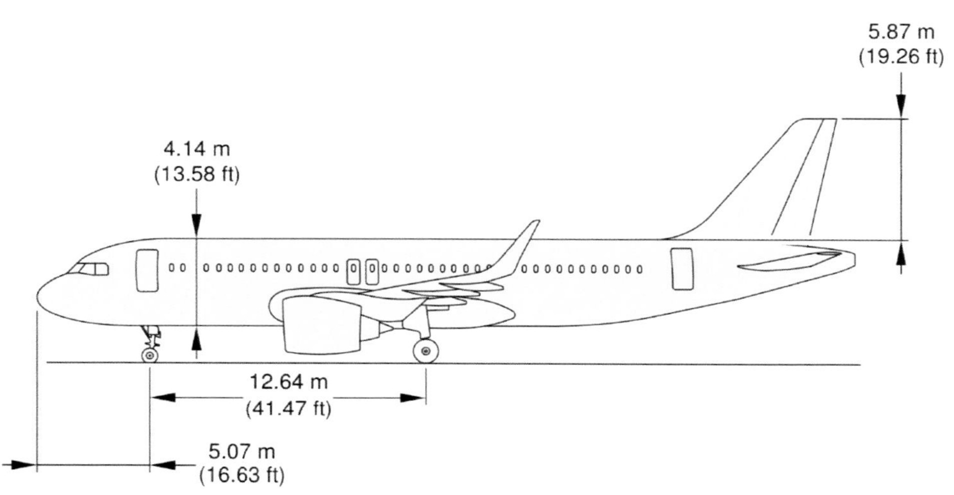

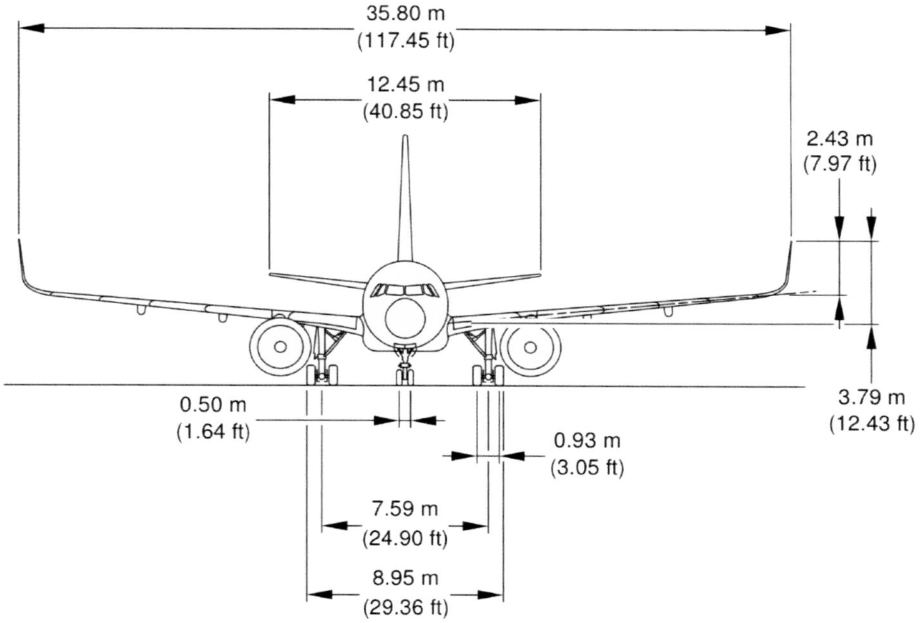

35.80 m
(117.45 ft)
12.45 m
(40.85 ft)
2.43 m
(7.97 ft)
0.50 m
(1.64 ft)
3.79 m
(12.43 ft)
0.93 m
(3.05 ft)
7.59 m
(24.90 ft)
8.95 m
(29.36 ft)

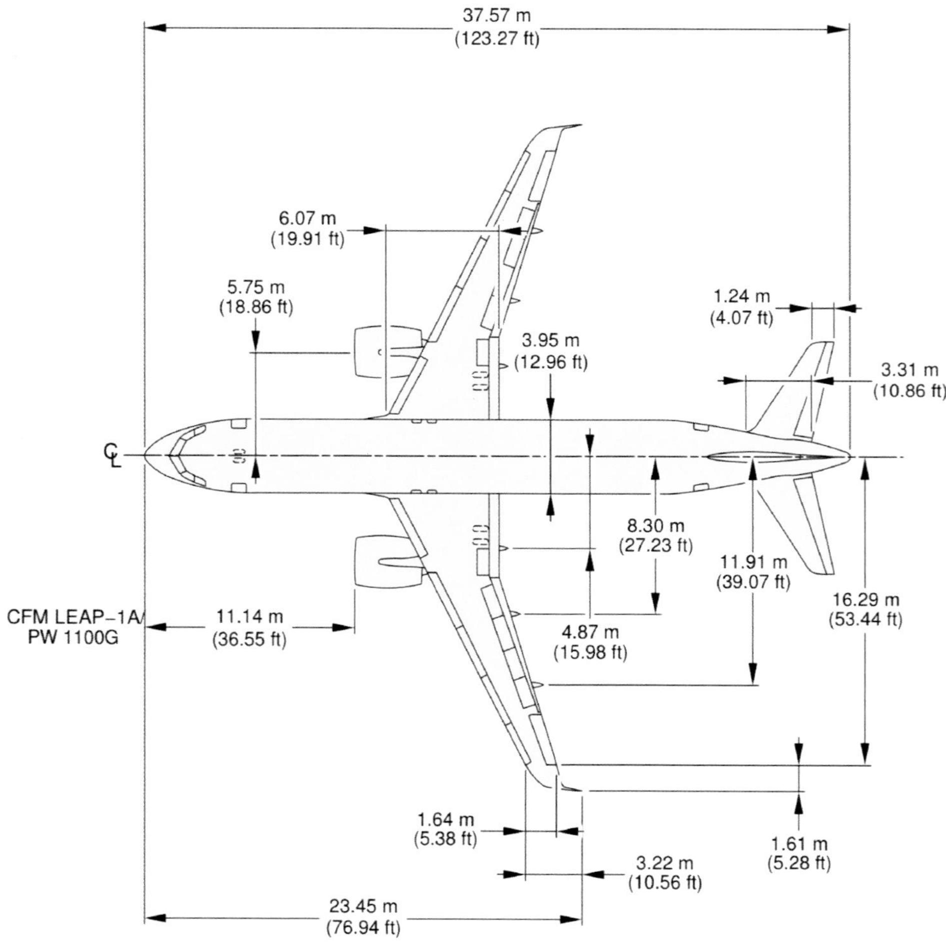

37.57 m
(123.27 ft)
6.07 m
(19.91 ft)
5.75 m
(18.86 ft)
1.24 m
(4.07 ft)
3.95 m
(12.96 ft)
3.31 m
(10.86 ft)
℄
8.30 m
(27.23 ft)
11.91 m
(39.07 ft)
16.29 m
(53.44 ft)
CFM LEAP–1A/
PW 1100G
11.14 m
(36.55 ft)
4.87 m
(15.98 ft)
1.64 m
(5.38 ft)
3.22 m
(10.56 ft)
1.61 m
(5.28 ft)
23.45 m
(76.94 ft)

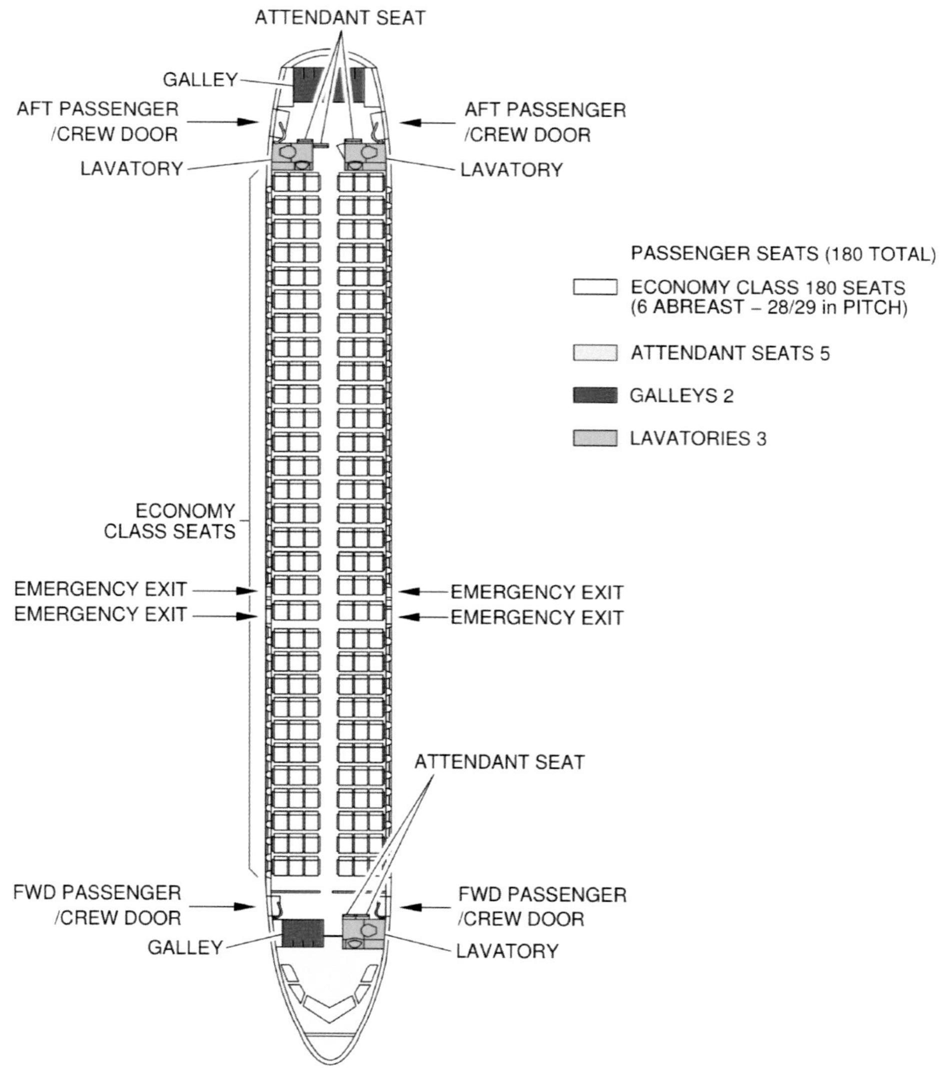
ATTENDANT SEAT
GALLEY
AFT PASSENGER /CREW DOOR
AFT PASSENGER /CREW DOOR
LAVATORY
LAVATORY
PASSENGER SEATS (180 TOTAL)
ECONOMY CLASS 180 SEATS (6 ABREAST – 28/29 in PITCH)
ATTENDANT SEATS 5
GALLEYS 2
LAVATORIES 3
ECONOMY CLASS SEATS
EMERGENCY EXIT
EMERGENCY EXIT
EMERGENCY EXIT
EMERGENCY EXIT
ATTENDANT SEAT
FWD PASSENGER /CREW DOOR
FWD PASSENGER /CREW DOOR
GALLEY
LAVATORY

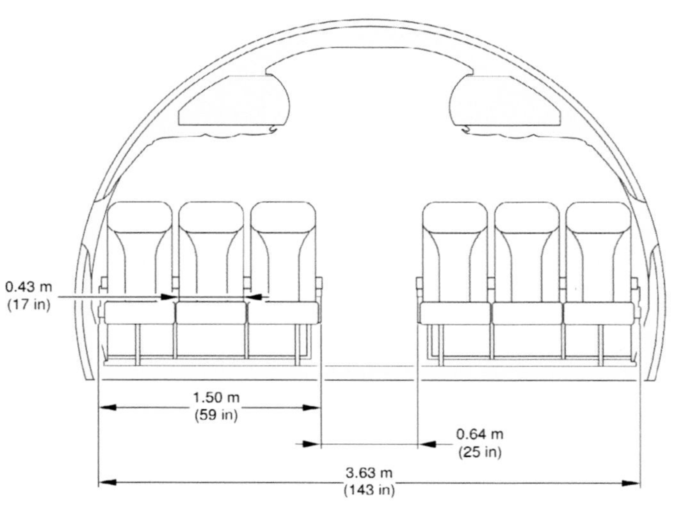

6 ABREAST-WIDER AISLE
0.43 m
(17 in)
1.50 m
(59 in)
0.64 m
(25 in)
3.63 m
(143 in)

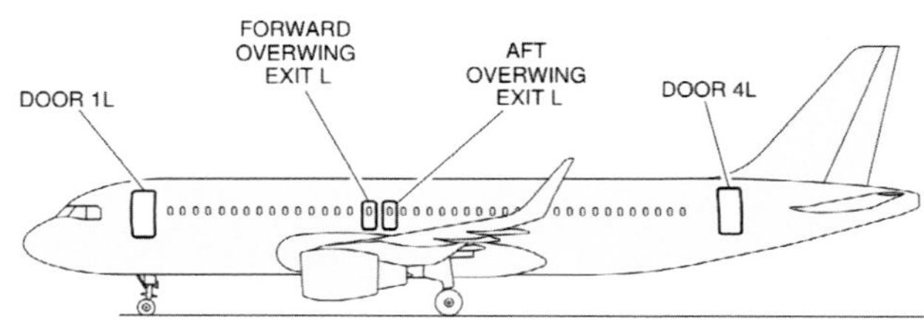

FORWARD
OVERWING
EXIT L
AFT
OVERWING
EXIT L
DOOR 1L
DOOR 4L

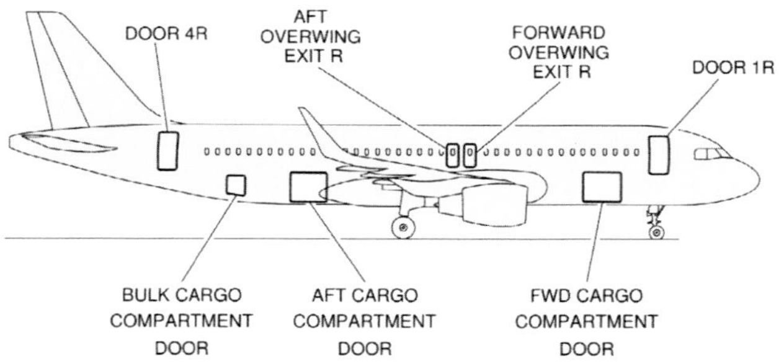

DOOR 4R
AFT
OVERWING
EXIT R
FORWARD
OVERWING
EXIT R
DOOR 1R
BULK CARGO
COMPARTMENT
DOOR
AFT CARGO
COMPARTMENT
DOOR
FWD CARGO
COMPARTMENT
DOOR

AIR CONDITIONING / VENTILATION / PRESSURISATION

Air Conditioning

The A320 air conditioning system allows fresh air into the aircraft via 2 packs (Pressurisation & conditioning kit), these are located on the lower fuselage.

The pneumatic system provides bleed air to the air conditioning packs via a pack flow control valve. This regulates the airflow to the associated pack and is controlled using the PACK 1 or PACK 2 pb.

Downstream of the of the pack flow control valve, the airflow can be selected using the PACK FLOW selector knob. This has 3 settings of LO, NORM and HI.

LO - 80% of normal flow – Upto 130 Passengers

NORM - 100% of normal flow - Normal operations.

HI - 120% of normal flow – Used in high temperature situations.

Pack Operation:

Hot bleed air from the engines is routed via the pack flow control valve to the primary heat exchanger, where it is then cooled by ambient ram air. This ambient air is supplied via the ram air inlet / outlet doors, both of which can be operated to increase or to decrease cooling.

The cooled bleed air is then compressed to a higher pressure and temperature, before being cooled again in the main heat exchanger. It then enters the turbine section where it expands, generating power to drive the compressor and also the cooling air fan. This process removes energy and thus greatly reduces the air temperature at the turbine discharge.

This cold air then enters a mixing unit where it is mixed with cabin air to increase airflow distribution. Air from the cabin is drawn into the mixing unit using two fans, these are continuously in use whilst electrical power is supplied. These fans can be controlled using the CAB FANS pb.

Bleed air is tapped upstream of the pack flow control valve to the pressure regulating valve. This hot air then flows to three trim air valves which are independently supplied to the fwd cabin, aft cabin and cockpit. This hot is air is used to regulate the temperature. These valves are controlled by the HOT AIR pb.

Temperature control can be regulated via 3 rotary selector knobs on the overhead panel. The temperature range is from 18°c to 30°c with a temperature of around 24°c being in the 12 o'clock position. Cabin crew can use the FAP to vary cabin temperature +/- 2.5°c from what has been selected in the cockpit.

Air Conditioning Schematic

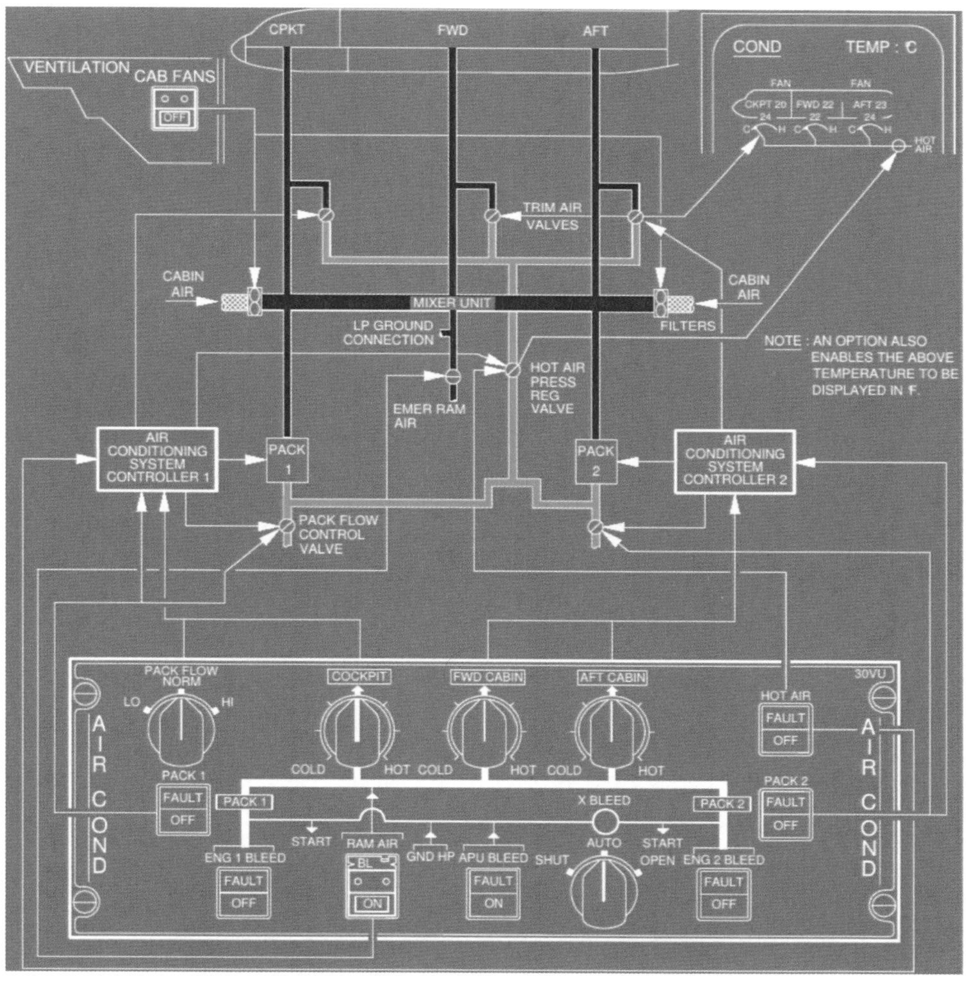

Emergency RAM Air

The RAM air inlet will ventilate the cabin and cockpit to remove smoke if required, or if both packs fail. This can be controlled by using the RAM AIR pb on the overhead panel. Providing the Ditching pb has not been selected, the RAM air valve will open.

Once pushed and if the cabin pressure is less than 1 PSI and under automatic operation, the Outflow valve will open to around 50%.

If the differential pressure is above 1 PSI, the RAM air inlet will remain in the closed position.

Ventilation

The ventilation system provides ventilation for the following:

- Aircraft avionics
- Batteries
- Lavatories & Galleys

The system is fully automatic and uses two electric fans to circulate the air, as well as air which is sucked in from the cockpit. These fans circulate air around the avionics compartment at a low / high speed depending on the temperature of the ventilation air. In order to allow air into the aircraft, valves called Skin air inlet and outlet valves allow ambient air inside, and warm air from the avionics compartment outside.

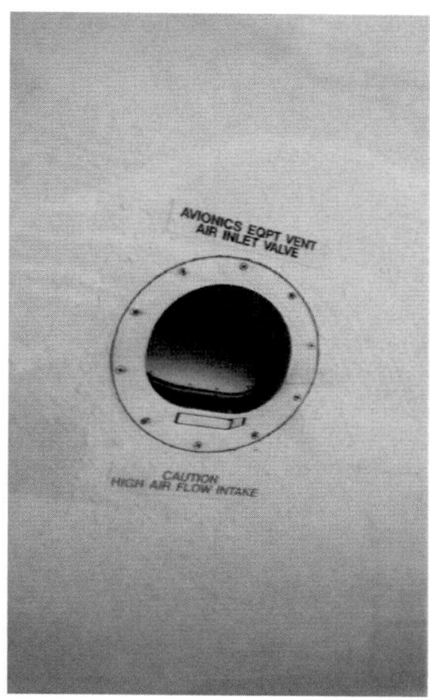

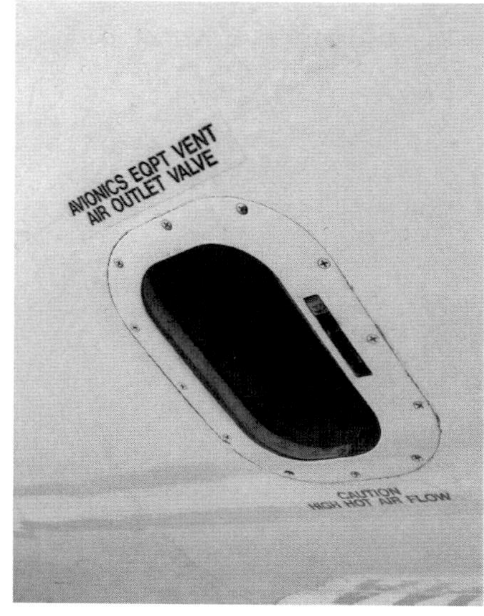

Skin exchange inlet / outlet valves allow air to circulate between the avionics bay and beneath the cargo compartment floor. The air conditioning inlet valve allows the air conditioning circuit to add fresh air to the avionics bay. A skin heat exchanger lies between the pressure hull and the outer aircraft skin. It uses the low temperature from the skin to assist with cooling.

The system is operated to provide cool air in 5 different ways:

Open circuit configuration - When the aircraft is on the ground, skin temperature above 12°c and increasing and thrust levers not in takeoff position. Ambient air goes past a valve then a filter before reaching the avionics rack to be cooled. Water particles and any dust or debris are removed at this stage.

Closed circuit configuration - Aircraft on the ground with skin temperature 9°c and decreasing, during takeoff and also inflight if the skin temperature is below 32°c and decreasing. Skin air inlet / outlet valves remain closed in this configuration.

Intermediate configuration - When the skin temperature is above 35°c and increasing whilst inflight.

Abnormal configuration - When the blower pb is set to OVRD, the blower fan stops and extract fan runs. When the extract pb is set to OVRD, the extract fan is controlled directly from the pb. Both fans will continue to run.

Smoke configuration - Blower and Extract pb/s set to OVRD. The air conditioning system supplies cooling air which is then exhausted overboard. The blower fans will stop.

Pressurisation

The A320 pressurisation system is controlled either automatically or manually.

In normal operation, the crew only need to monitor the pressurisation system. Internal air pressure is scheduled via signals received from the FMGS. If the FMGS fails (dual FMGC failure) the crew need to manually set the landing elevation.

2 cabin pressure controllers (CPC) control the system using data from the ADIRS (Pressure altitude), FMGC (landing elevation and QNH), EIU and LGCIU. In normal operation one controller is in use, the other in standby. A changeover occurs 70 s after landing and, if one system fails.

Cabin Pressurisation Functions	
Ground Function	Fully opens Outflow Valve when on ground 5 seconds after landing
Pre-Pressurisation	During takeoff, cabin pressure is increased at around 400 ft/min to avoid a surge in pressure
Pressurisation in flight	Adjusts cabin altitude and rate of change. Max descent rate is 750 ft/min
Depressurisation	On touchdown, gradually releases residual cabin pressure before the ground function fully opens the Outflow valve

3 electric motors power the outflow valve. In normal operation, one of two cabin pressure controllers operates the outflow valve via a motor. An auto transfer occurs 70 seconds after each landing or if the operating system fails.

Cabin altitude can be controlled manually using the manual motor which also controls the outflow valve.

Ditching pb - closes the outflow valve, emergency ram air inlet, avionics ventilation inlet and extract valves, pack flow control valve and the fwd cargo outlet isolation valve.

If the cabin becomes over pressurised, 2 independent safety valves can relieve the pressure once it gets close to 8.6 PSI. These valves are located on the rear pressure bulkhead.

Automatic Pressure Control

The controller will automatically control the cabin pressure and will limit this to around 8000 ft during cruise.

Landing Elevation and QNH Information is taken from the FMGC, whilst the pressure altitude is taken from ADIRS.

If there is a dual FMGC failure and no information is available, the Captain BARO reference is used as well as the manually selected LDG ELEV from the overhead panel.

Pressurisation Modes	
Ground	Before takeoff and 55 seconds after landing, outflow valve is fully opened. At touchdown, remaining pressure is released at 500 ft/min
Takeoff	Pre-pressurises the aircraft at around 400 ft/min until pressure reaches 0.1 PSI. At liftoff the controller initiates Climb phase.
Climb	The cabin altitude varies, taking into account the aircraft's actual rate of climb vs a pre-programmed law.
Cruise	Controller will maintain cabin altitude at level off altitude, or landing field elevation whichever is higher. Cabin altitude limited to around 8000ft.
Descent	The controller maintains a rate of descent so cabin pressure equals landing airfield pressure + 0.1 PSI just before landing. Max descent rate is 750 ft/min.
Abort	If the aircraft does not climb after takeoff, cabin altitude will be prevented from climbing. Cabin pressure reset to 0.1 PSI.

Limitations	
Max Positive Differential Pressure	9.0 PSI
Max Negative Differential Pressure	-1.0 PSI
Safety Relief Valve Operation	8.6 PSI
Max Norm Cabin Altitude	8000 ft
Cabin Altitude Warning	9550 ft +/- 35 ft
Ram Air Max Diff	1 PSI

More than 20 minutes without air conditioning will reduce the quality of the air within the cabin and is not advised.

On the ground and depending on outside air temperature, crews must limit the time the electrical power supply is used in normal avionics configuration. This only applies to very hot airports.	
OAT less than 49°C	No Limitation
49°C - 55°C	2 Hrs
55°C - 60°C	1 Hr
60°C - 64°C	0.5 Hrs

Questions & Answers

Q. How is temperature regulated by the air conditioning system?
A. Both air conditioning pack outlets feed into the mixing unit. The output temperature of the packs is driven by the lowest selected of the 3 zonal temperature controllers, so that air within the mixer unit will be equal to that lowest selected temperature. As air is ducted to the 3 zones, hot air is added via the trim air valves to optimise zonal temperatures.

Q. What do the trim air valves do?
A. Add hot air to the cool air ducted in to the cabin to optimise the cabin air temperature.

Q. How many air conditioning controllers are there and what do they control?
A. There are 2 air conditioning controllers. Controller 1 controls pack 1 and vice versa. Controller 1 controls cockpit temperature and controller 2 controls both cabin zones. The controllers allow the air conditioning system to be fully automatic. They control the pack control valve, the trim air valves and the pack outlet temperature via the pack turbine bypass valve.

Q. What is the purpose of the ram air inlet and when will it be opened if pressed?
A. It enables the cabin to be supplied with fresh air in the event of smoke or loss of both packs. It is activated via a guarded pb on the overhead panel. The valve will open automatically when pushed, however the cabin differential pressure must be below 1psi (otherwise no air will be supplied). Ram air pb shall not be selected until FL100 or below. Once pushed, the outflow valve will open to approximately 50% and the ram air door will open. If the pressure diff is above 1psi, a check valve downstream will not open and no air will be supplied - i.e. atmospheric ram air can only be used in a depressurised aircraft.

Q. Where are the 3 zonal temperatures measured?
A. Cockpit - behind the FO seat. Cabin zones - lavatory extraction system and the galleys.

Q. What occurs if an air conditioning controller suffers a single or dual channel failure?
A. The air conditioning controller will still function with a single lane failure. A dual lane failure will cause the loss of the controller.

Q. What happens if a hot air valve fails?
A. If it fails in the open position, there is no effect. If it fails in the closed position, the trim air valves will not be supplied, so temperature control of the cabin is lost.

Q. What happens if a trim air valve closes?
A. Temperature control is lost in that cabin zone

Q. The ram air inlet flaps automatically close under two conditions, what are they?
A. Takeoff - T/O power set and MLG struts compressed Landing - MLG struts compressed, speed greater than 70kts

Q. What is the ACSC and what does it do?
A. Air conditioning system controller. Each ACSC regulates the temperature of its associated pack by modulating the bypass valve and ram air inlet flap. It has the following functions: • Controls pack flow control valve • Controls hot air pressure regulating valve • Controls trim air valve • Regulates temperature and flow

Q. What is pre pressurisation mode?
A. Active during the takeoff roll, the outflow valve moves towards a closed position, the pressure in the cabin then increases to 0.1psi above ambient to avoid a cabin surge during rotation.

Q. When do de-pressurisation and ground modes activate and what happens in automatic mode?
A. De-pressurisation mode occurs on touchdown which releases any cabin overpressure. Ground mode occurs 5 seconds after landing at which point the outflow valve fully opens.

Q. What is the maximum cabin altitude in automatic mode?
A. 8000 ft

Q. What does the pressurisation system use in automatic mode as a reference for landing elevation?
A. The destination QNH from the PERF APPR page and the airfield elevation from FMGC.

Q. How is manual pressurisation achieved and how does it work?
A. By using the manual override pb on the overhead panel. The third motor for manual mode is now energised. Manual control is achieved through a dedicated part of the CPC1 which remains available even in dual CPC failure. Cabin altitude is controlled using the toggle switch which adjusts the position of the outflow valve. Pressurisation will now be displayed by ECAM.

Q. What pressurisation procedures are available in the QRH?
A. Cabin Overpressure - Should be initiated as soon as control is lost of the pressurisation system, leading to over pressurisation. This is usually due to a loss of control of the outflow valve. A simple solution to this is to turn off the packs, then turning the blower and extract to override will vent cabin air overboard. Now the pressure can be monitored and by selecting the packs on/off, there remains a way of controlling the pressure.

Outflow Valve

CAB PR SYS 1+2 FAULT

- Manual control of pressurisation required
- Achieved by selecting MODE SEL to MAN and using manual toggle switch to operate the outflow valve.
- Toggle down - closes outflow valve - cabin altitude descends
- Toggle up - opens outflow valve - cabin altitude climbs

Target cabin v/s is:

500 ft/min Climb

300 ft/min Descent

Threats:

- Over pressurisation (resulting in the operation of the safety valves)
- Under pressurisation (resulting in CAB PR EXCESS CAB ALT)

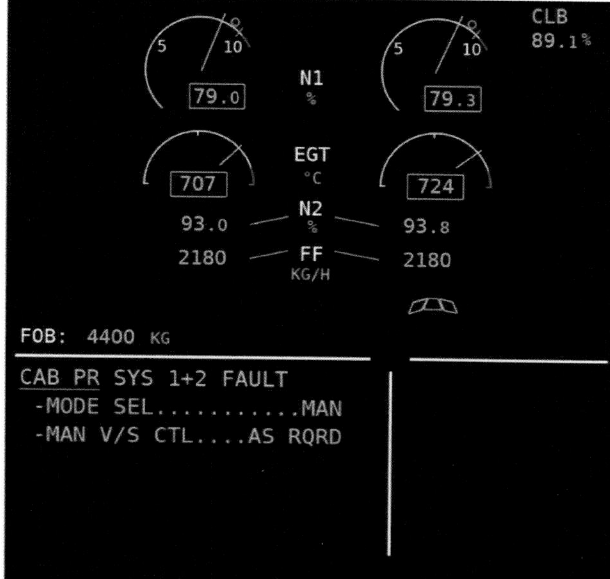

Flying at lower levels will enable easier control of the cabin altitude / differential pressure.

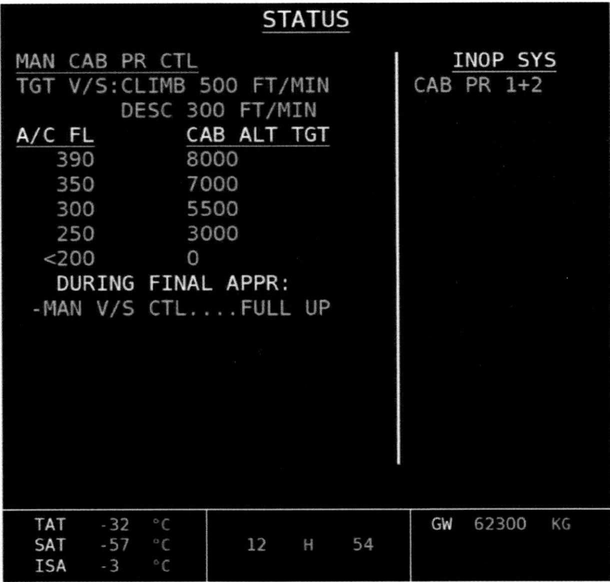

Strategy 1

Maintain a cabin v/s of 300 ft/min in the descent. If a level off is required, ensure v/s 0. Maintain cabin altitude between destination altitude and 8000 ft, pressure between zero and 8psi. During final approach, fully open outflow valve.

Strategy 2

Maintain the cabin altitude at its original value, e.g. 8000 ft. Descend down to 8000 ft and once reached, the outflow valve can be fully opened. This provides less management of the system manually. Once below 8000 ft however, ensure that the v/s does not exceed 1800 ft/min otherwise the ADV will be shown.

Cabin Overpressure

This failure requires the pilots to reduce cabin pressure to avoid any further over-pressure.

- Select PACK 1 or 2 OFF
- Ventilation Blower - Override
- Ventilation Extract - Override

This will put the aircraft in the smoke removal configuration which moves cabin air overboard and reduces airflow into the cabin.

Monitor the cabin pressure, if it goes above 9 psi, then turn off the remaining pack

As cabin pressurisation is now unreliable, LAND ASAP appears requiring an expeditious descent.

Landing
10 minutes prior to landing, both packs - OFF
Return ventilation system back to the normal configuration
Check cabin pressure is zero prior to opening cabin doors

CAB PR EXCESS CAB ALT

Time of useful consciousness at FL390 is in the region of 15 seconds. The physiological experience will be unpleasant. The flight deck visibility will be reduced and pain will be felt in the ears.

- Immediately don oxygen masks to prevent incapacitation
- Ensure positive confirmation CAB PR EXCESS CAB ALT
- Initiate emergency descent

Immediate Actions	
ALT	Turn & Pull
HDG	Turn & Pull
Speed	Pull
FMA	Announce
Refine FCU Selections - Note MSA..	

  - Memory items
  - QRH
  - ECAM

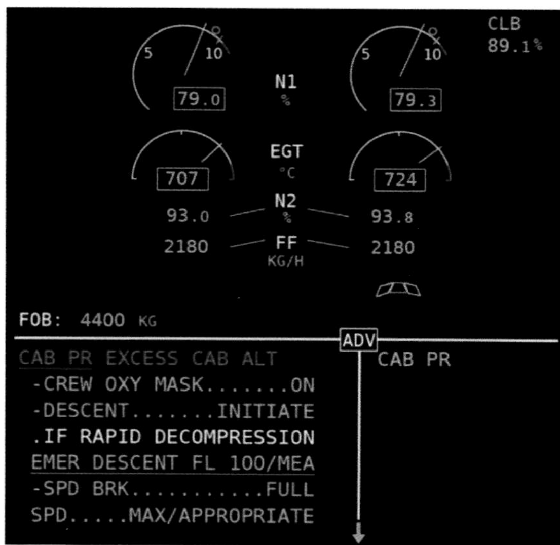

Threats
Ensure situational awareness is maintained - Check MSA
Selected Heading - Aircraft below?
Advise ATC, Squawk 7700 when able
Use of autopilot / autothrust highly recommended
If no structural damage, use speedbrakes to expedite descent - monitor VLS increase
In Idle thrust with speedbrakes extended, rate of descent is approx. 7000 fpm. Descent from FL 390 to FL 100 will take approx. 4 minutes and 40 nm.
If cabin altitude goes above 14,000 ft, press MASK MAN OK pb. This ensures passenger oxygen masks are released.

Once below FL100, the flight crew should then reduce the vertical rate of descent to around 1000 ft per minute.

Now the aircraft is in a safe condition, it is time to further diagnose the problem and if not already done so, establish some diversion options close to you.

The cabin crew and passengers are likely to be in a poor condition so communication at this stage is vital to establish the state of the cabin / damage / passengers.

This warning is usually due to a structural failure so although it is vital to be on the ground as soon as possible, care must be taken to not over stress the airframe and consider all viable options for airport facilities.

ELECTRICAL

The A320 electrical system is powered by an AC and DC electrical system. This is structured into two independent 'networks' which can be called No. 1 and No. 2. Should there be a failure of both systems there is a backup network referred to as the Essential network.

On each engine is an AC generator, which is driven via a gearbox from the high pressure spool. Also connected to this gearbox is the constant speed drive (CSD). This converts the variable output speed of the engine to a constant generator speed of around 1200rpm. The generator and the CSD are co-located in one place situated under the engine, this is called the Integrated drive generator (IDG). The generators supply 115V / 200V at 400Hz.

There is a third generator powered by the Auxiliary Power Unit (APU). Each of these generators is capable of supplying power for the entire aircraft and is automatically brought on line according to their priority.

Electrical priority:

1 - Generators

2 - External power

3 - APU Generator

4 - Ram Air Turbine

5 - Batteries

There are 2 batteries provided for DC power with a minimum voltage of 25.5V. Should the voltage drop below this value, the batteries can be connected to the battery bus and external power applied for around 20 minutes. As a last resort, the batteries can supply up to 30 minutes of electrical power.

Batteries are permanently connected to the two hot buses and each has a battery charge limiter. Normal capacity is around 23 Ah.

Batteries are located beneath the front galley close to the avionics outlet valve.

If AC BUS 1 & 2 are lost, the Ram Air Turbine (RAT) automatically deploys, powering the blue hydraulic system which is then capable of powering an emergency AC generator. This then supplies AC ESS BUS and DC ESS BUS via the ESS TR. RAT extension takes around 8 seconds.

If the RAT stalls or below 100 kts on the ground, a static inverter supplies power to part of the AC essential bus as the batteries are the only remaining power source.

With the Rat deployed, a minimum speed of 140 kts must be maintained to prevent stalling. Below 50 kts, AC ESS BUS is automatically shed, all displays will be lost.

ON
CAPT
EMER ELEC PWR
EMER GEN TEST
RAT
&
EMER GEN
MAN ON
GEN 1 LINE
AUTO
GPWS
TERR
SYS
G/S
MODE
FLAP
MODE
LDG
FLAP 3

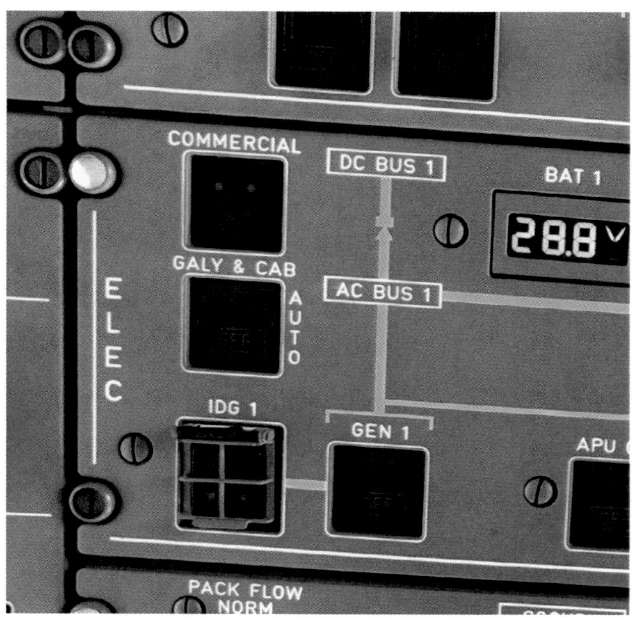
COMMERCIAL
DC BUS 1
BAT 1
28.8 V
GALY & CAB
AUTO
AC BUS 1
ELEC
IDG 1
GEN 1
APU
PACK FLOW
NORM

The aircraft has two types of Circuit Breakers.

GREEN	These are monitored. When out for greater than 1 minute, the ELEC C/B TRIPPED warning will appear on ECAM
BLACK	Non monitored

The CLR pb can be used to clear the ECAM C/B TRIPPED caution. If the pilots have pulled the CB, any additional tripped circuits on that same panel will not be detected and the ECAM will not display the caution. If the CB is pushed, the ECAM will detect a further trip and display on ECAM.

The EMER CANC pb will clear and inhibit the caution for the remainder of the flight.

Wing Tip Brake CB's have red caps on them which prevents a reset being performed.

What is an IDG?

The Integrated Drive Generator (IDG) uses the power from the engines to and converts it into electrical power for the aircraft. This is done using a constant speed drive which converts the variable input from the engine, into a constant speed for the generator to produce a fixed frequency and operate the electrical system efficiently.

Oil within the unit is used for cooling and lubrication, also to regulate the rotation speed of the generator.

Recirculated fuel is also used to cool the IDG. This is pumped via the HP fuel line into the IDG heat exchanger which helps at high oil temperatures or at low engine power. This process also warms the fuel which is circulated back to the fuel tanks.

The IDG pb is a red guarded switch, pressing it is an irreversible action. Do not press for longer than 3 seconds as this may damage the disconnection mechanism. This should only be pushed when the engine is running or windmilling.

Normal Operation:

Generator 1 supplies AC BUS 1, Generator 2 supplies AC BUS 2.

The AC ESS Bus is supplied by AC Bus 1.

TR1 supplies DC Bus 1, DC ESS Bus and the battery bus.

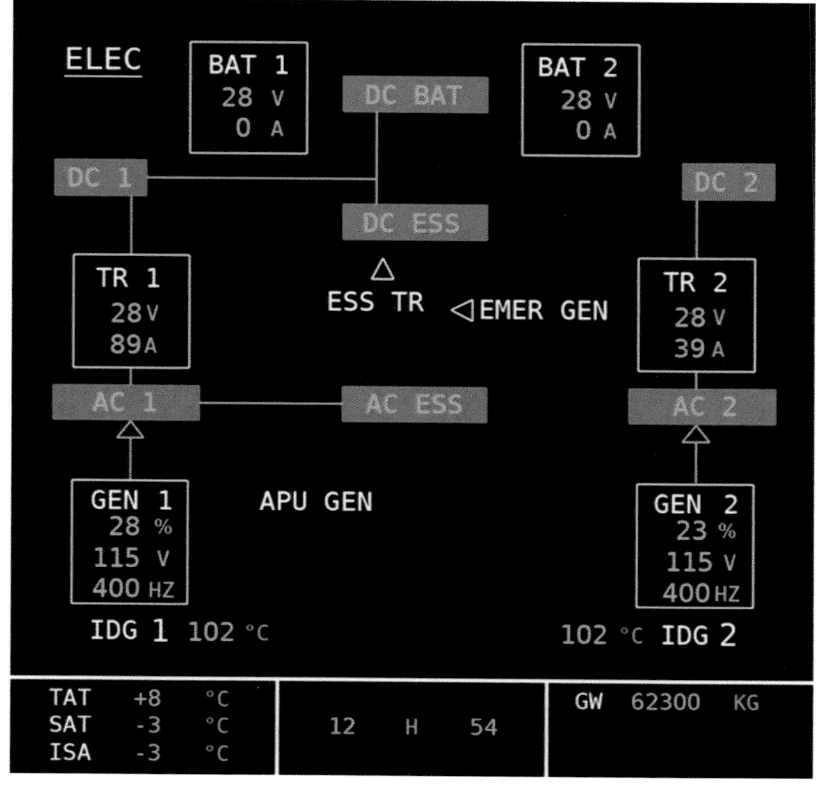

Abnormal Operation:

If an engine fails and the generator is lost, power will be used from the other generator.

If both generators fail, AC BUS 1 & 2 are lost.

The RAT will automatically deploy if the aircraft speed is above 100 kts.

After around 8 seconds, this powers the blue HYD system which in turn powers the emergency generator. It powers the AC ESS Bus, ESS TR, and the DC ESS BUS.

When the aircrafts speed drops below 100kts, AC SHED ESS and DC SHED ESS buses are shed and the batteries now power the essential system with the static inverter.

When on the ground, the DC BUS is automatically connected to the batteries below 100 kts.

Below 50 kts, the AC ESS BUS is shed.

Commercial pb - Supplies electrical power to:

- Cabin & Cargo lights
- Water & toilet system
- Drain mast ice protection
- Galley
- Semi-automatic cargo loading

Questions & Answers

Q. What is the output of the electrical system in normal operation?
A. 90KVA, 115-200V plus a 28v battery system

Q. What is the Bus Tie?
A. Enables power to be transferred from one side to another, thus enabling the APU to power both sides 1 & 2. Also, in the emergency electrical configuration, the system can be spilt to try to restore either sides power supply.

Q. What is the output of the Emergency Generator?
A. 5KVA

Q. What types of circuit breakers are there?
A. Monitored and unmonitored. Monitored are green and when tripped, after 1 minute an ECAM caution appears. Unmonitored are black and do not trigger any ECAM warnings. Wing tip brake CB's have a red collar to prevent these being reset inflight.

Q. What is the major consequence of a TR 1 & 2 failure?
A. DC Bus 1 & 2 failure

Q. How is electricity generated in abnormal situations?
A. The Emergency Generator, powered by the RAT, can supply 5KVA AC power. This powers the AC essential bus and the DC essential through the essential TR.

Q. In flight and on battery power only, what do the batteries supply?
A. Battery 1 supplies AC essential via the static inverter. Battery 2 supplies the DC essential bus.

Q. When will the electrical system be powered by only the batteries?
A. If AC bus 1 & 2 fail then the RAT will be deployed. This process takes 7-10 seconds before the generator comes on line and in this time, the batteries supply power.

Q. When completing the cockpit preparation checklist, a battery check is required. To do this, the batteries are switched off, and the battery voltage should indicate how many volts?
A. 25.5 Volts

Q. After starting ENG 2, which generator is powering AC BUS 1?
A. APU GEN

Q. What does the amber FAULT light on BAT pb indicate?
A. Charging current for the corresponding battery is outside limits. The battery contactor opens.

Q. What does the green AVAIL light on the EXT PWR pb mean?
A. External power is plugged in and the parameters are normal

Q. Can the APU Generator power all the buses in flight?
A. Yes it can

Failures

ELEC EMER CONFIG

Threats:

- Aviate / Navigate / Communicate
- Captain takes control as the FO has no screens or instrumentation
- AP, ATHR disconnect, assume manual flight - FD off, Bird on.

Threats
To confirm the failure, press and hold the ELEC pb on the ECP
Reset both generators in order to try to establish power. BUS TIE is selected OFF in order to segregate both generator channels, then try the resets again.
IGN - ON as both engines now gravity fuel feeding. As descent will most likely be initiated, QRH gravity feeding procedure can be referenced but is not a priority.
VHF1 only so Captain to make all radio calls.
FAC 1 reset will restore the rudder trim function.
Starting the APU is delayed for 45 seconds after loss of both generators to prevent interference with coupling.
Starting the APU on batteries is restricted to FL250
Setting the Blower and Extract to OVRD assists in avionics ventilation

F/CTRL ALTN LAW - Max Speed 320 kts due to loss of high speed protection

AUTO FLT A/THR OFF - Move thrust levers out of thrust lock and assume manual control, reset the original N1's.

Now that all ECAM actions have been completed, the pilots can decide what to do. This can be in the format of DODAR or any other failure management models.

The QRH summary page provides an excellent overview. The following should be considered when deciding on a suitable airfield:

- CAT 1 weather
- Long runway - ideally 3000m
- Minimal terrain implications
- Emergency cover (RFFS) / facilities

Approach & Landing	
RA 1 & 2 both lost	Auto call-outs made by PM
Min Approach Speed 140 kts	Ensures RAT supplies Emer Gen
When Gear down -	Aircraft in Direct Law
BSCU is lost	Nosewheel Steering & Alternate braking on Y system No Antiskid
Slats / Flaps slow	Extra time to configure
Reversers not available	Landing distance calculation
Only 2 spoilers per wing	
N/W Steering inop	Cannot vacate runway

When passing 50 kts on the landing roll, the display units will be lost.

EMER ELEC Configuration

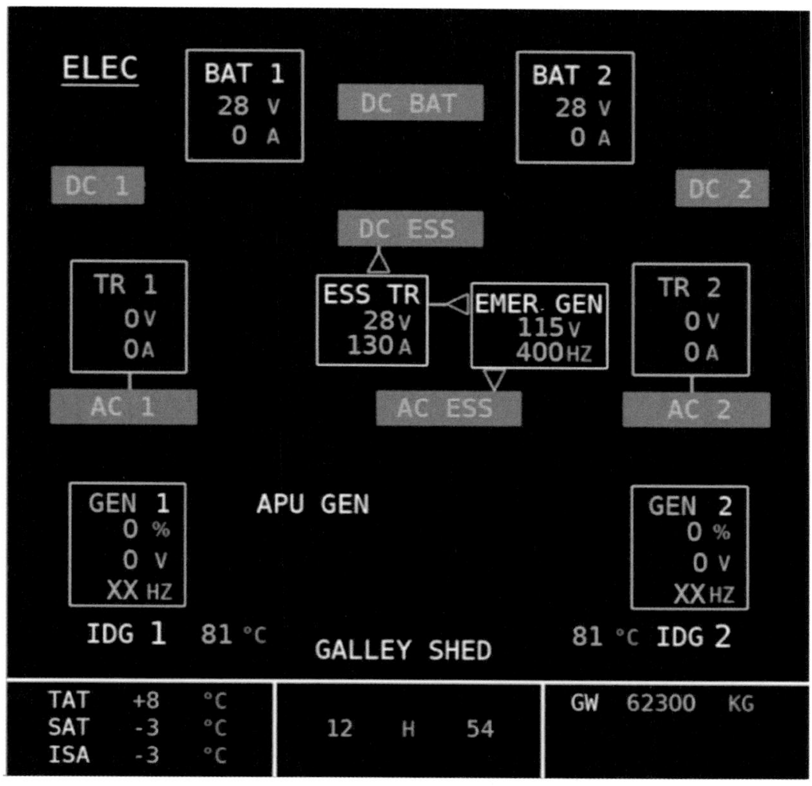

ELEC DC ESS BUS FAULT

Threats
Aviate / Navigate / Communicate
AP Will disconnect if AP 1 is active - AP 2 is available
A/THR disconnects - move thrust levers to get out of thrust lock and regain manual control
Both loudspeakers are inop until ACP switching, then CM2 speaker will work
RMP 1 inop, tune current frequency on RMP 2
Audio switching to F/O 3 enables both pilots to hear RT comms with the speaker turned up on CM 2 side
Loss of fuel pumps on older A319's, newer aircraft not affected

- Blue HYD pump inop - triangles remain green on HYD SD page therefore system pressure remains suitable.
- CAT 3 Single displayed - actual capability remains CAT 2 when APP pb selected
- HP fuel shutoff valves are inop - engines shut down using the ENG fire pb's - this can take upto 1 minute before the fuel in the line is used.

Approach & Landing	
Slats / Flaps slow	Extra time to configure
Reverser 2 inop	Landing Distance calculation
SPLR 3 inop	
GPWS	Greater terrain awareness

With AP2 engaged and comms re-established, there is time to manage this scenario with no need to rush.

ELEC AC BUS 1 FAULT

- Aircraft will automatically switch AC ESS to AC2
- DC ESS is supplied via the ESS TR
- AC1 and TR 1 are both lost
- DC BUS 2 supplies DC BUS 1and DC BAT BUS after 5 seconds

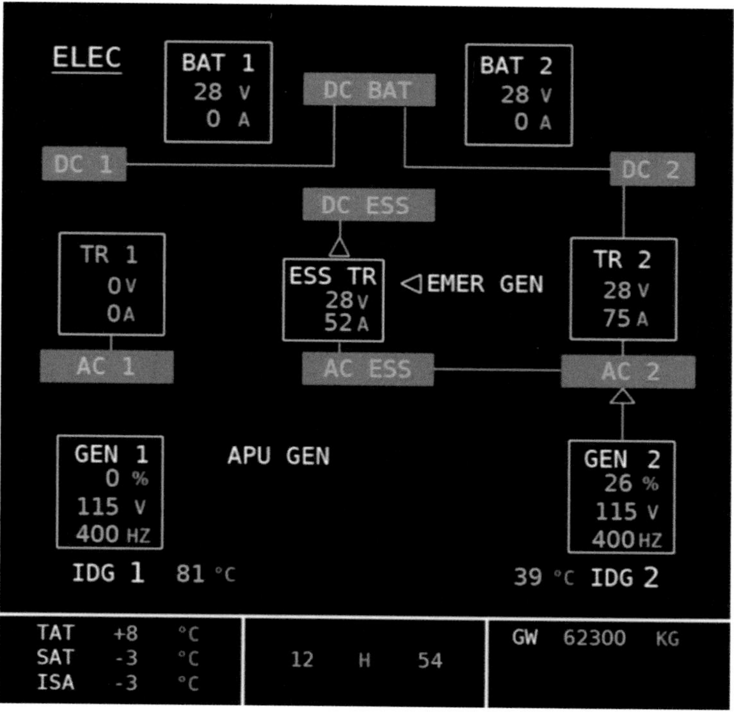

Approach & Landing	
CAT 2 ONLY	CAT I weather required
Slats Slow	No major implication
N.W STEER	Unable to vacate runway after landing

FIRE PROTECTION

The engines and APU have a fire and an overheat detection system which includes:

- 2 detection loops A & B
- Fire detection unit

The detection loop consists of sensing elements in the pylon nacelle, the engine core and also in the engine fan section.

The APU consists of 1 sensing element.

As soon as heat is detected above a preset level, a fire warning system is triggered. If one loop has a fault, it does not affect the other.

Each engine has 2 fire extinguisher bottles, each with electrically controlled squibs used to discharge agents.

The APU has 1 fire extinguisher bottle with 2 squibs to discharge the agent. If an APU fire is detected on the ground, the APU will automatically shut down and the extinguisher will automatically discharge.

When the ENG 1(2) FIRE pb is pushed, the following occurs:

- Silences the aural fire warning
- Arms the fire extinguisher squibs
- Closes the low pressure fuel valve
- Closes the hydraulic fire shutoff valve
- Closes the engine bleed valve
- Closes the pack flow control valve
- Cuts of the FADEC power supply
- Deactivates the IDG

Both AGENT pb switches of the selected affected engine will be active when the FIRE pb is released.

SQUIB will illuminate in white to assist the pilots to identify the AGENT pb to be selected.

DISCH illuminates in amber when the selected fire extinguisher has lost pressure.

When the APU FIRE pb is pushed, the following occurs:

- Shuts down the APU
- Silences the aural warning
- Arms squib on the APU fire extinguisher
- Closes the low pressure fuel valve
- Shuts off the APU fuel pump
- Closes the APU bleed valve and X bleed valve and deactivates APU generator

The FWD and AFT cargo compartments have smoke detection systems consisting of 2 detectors in the FWD and 4 in the AFT compartments

There consists of 1 fire bottle with 2 discharge heads, one for each compartment. One nozzle is in the FWD compartment, two nozzles in the AFT compartment.

After activation, the DISCH light comes on in amber when the bottle is empty.

Most fire protection systems are designed to dilute the surrounding atmosphere with an inert agent that will not combust. The most common agent used on aircraft is Halon 1301 due to its effective capability and its low toxicity.

Halon production has ceased in many countries now due to evidence suggesting that it contributed to stratospheric ozone layer depletion. Until this replacement recycled Halon is still currently used with many airlines.

Q. How is fire detected in the engines and APU?
A. Detection works in a loop system which is ran in parallel. The Engines and APU have 2 loops. Heat detectors detect abnormally high temperatures and both loops need to detect this to signal a fire.

Q. How is fire detected in the engines and APU?
A. Detection works in a loop system which is ran in parallel. The Engines and APU have 2 loops. Heat detectors detect abnormally high temperatures and both loops need to detect this to signal a fire.

Q. Where are fire loops located on the engine?
A. Nacelle, Pylon, Core & Fan

Q. Is there a fire extinguisher in the hold?
A. There is one bottle that can be discharged for all 3 holds via pipes and nozzles. The bottle can be discharged in up to 1 minute.

Q. How is fire detected in the Avionics Bay?
A. If smoke is detected for 5 seconds or more, a smoke detector causes a fire warning chime. This smoke can only be removed using the QRH smoke removal checklist.

Q. What happens if the APU fire pb is pushed?
• The APU is shut down • LP fuel valve is closed • APU fuel pump deactivated • Aural warning silenced • Squibs armed • APU Bleed & Cross bleed valves closed • APU Generator is de-activated

Q. What happens when the ENG 1/2 FIRE TEST pb is pressed?
• Repetitive continuous chime sounds • MASTER WARNING lights flash • ENG FIRE warning appears on ECAM On the fire panel: ENG 1/2 FIRE pb lights up red SQUIB lights come on white if discharge supplies avail DISCH lights come on amber On the ENG MASTER panel: FIRE lights come on in red

FLIGHT CONTROLS

Flight control surfaces are all electrically controlled and hydraulically activated. The A320 has 11 computers that transfer the pilot / AP inputs to mechanical movements. These include:

2 x Elevator Aileron Computer (ELAC)

Control the Elevators, Trimable horizontal stabiliser (THS) and the Ailerons.

3 x Spoiler Elevator Computer (SEC)

Control the inputs for Spoilers and also backup for the elevators and THS

2 x Flight Augmentation Computer (FAC)

Controls the Rudder, including rudder trim and yaw dampening. It also provides windshear detection and low energy warnings.

2 x Slat Flap Control Computers (SFCC)

Control the flaps and slats on the wing.

2 x Flight Control Data Concentrators (FCDC)

Send data from the SEC's and the ELAC's directly to the ECAM.

Sidesticks

The sidestick is not mechanically linked and does not receive feedback from flight control surfaces. Pilot inputs are sent to the ELACS and SECs which in turn send signals to the primary flight controls. If both are moved at the same time, the inputs are added together to the maximum deflection and SIDESTICK PRIORITY lights up in front of both pilots with a verbal 'DUAL INPUT' call through the loudspeaker.

If a pilot presses the red AP disconnect / takeover pb for longer than 40 seconds, the other sidestick is deactivated.

A Red arrow light comes on in front of the pilot whose sidestick is deactivated.

A Green light comes on in front of the pilot who has taken control.

Roll Control

One Aileron and 4 Spoilers on each wing control the roll.

	A319 / A320	A321 NEO
Max Aileron deflection	25°	25°
Aileron extension when flaps extended (Aileron droop)	5°	10°
Max deflection of Spoilers	35°	35° Spoilers 2, 4 and 7 7° Spoilers 3

ELAC 1 will normally control the ailerons. If ELAC 1 fails then ELAC 2 is automatically used. If both ELAC's fail then the ailerons will revert to damping mode.

SEC's control the spoilers and if a SEC fails, the spoilers under its control will automatically retract.

Aileron Actuation - Each aileron has two electrically controlled hydraulic servojacks. Each has two control modes.

Active	Jack position is electronically controlled
Damping	Jack follows the surface movement

Spoilers receive hydraulic power from either the green, blue or yellow systems controlled by SEC 1, 2 or 3.

Spoilers automatically revert to their zero position if a fault is detected, or electrical power lost. Should hydraulic power be lost, the spoiler will retain the deflection it had at the time of the loss, however aerodynamic pressure could limit this deflection.

If a spoiler fails on one wing, the symmetric one on the other wing is inhibited.

Speed Brakes / Spoilers

5 spoilers on the upper side of the wing are used to function as roll spoilers, ground spoilers and Speedbrakes. The Speedbrakes are operated by using the speedbrake lever which in turn activates spoilers 2, 3 & 4.

Speedbrake extension is inhibited when:

- Sec 1 / SEC 3 both faulty
- L or R elevator fault
- Angle of Attack protection active
- Flaps in config FULL
- Thrust levers above MCT
- Alpha floor activation

If one of the above occurs whilst the speedbrakes are extended, they will automatically retract and stay retracted until the condition ceases.

When flying faster than 315 kt / M 0.75, speedbrake retraction rate is reduced to 25 seconds from full to clean.

Max Deflection in Manual Flight			
	A319	**A320**	**A321**
Spoilers 3 & 4	25°	40°	25°
Spoilers 2	17.5°	20°	25°
	12.5° Config 3		

Max Deflection in Automatic Flight			
	A319	**A320**	**A321**
Spoilers 3 & 4	25°	25°	25°
Spoilers 2	17.5°	12.5°	25°

Ground Spoilers

Involves all 5 spoilers and ailerons. This is armed by pulling the speedbrake lever up into the armed position.

Rejected takeoff

- If armed and the aircraft speed exceeds 72 kt, the spoilers will automatically extend when both thrust levers are set to idle.
- If they are not armed but the speed exceeds 72 kt, the spoilers automatically extend as soon as reverse thrust is selected on one engine.

Landing Phase

The ground spoilers will automatically extend when the following conditions occur:

- Ground spoilers armed
- Both main landing gears on the ground
- Both thrust levers at / below idle, or reverse thrust selected on 1 engine.
- Ground spoilers not armed
- Both main landing gears on the ground
- Reverse thrust selected on at least one engine.

Ground Spoiler Retraction

- After a landing
- During a touch and go when one thrust lever is above 20°
- After a rejected takeoff and when ground spoilers disarmed

Phased Lift Dumping allows the spoilers to deploy at a reduced deflection in order to accelerate full spoiler deflection. The following conditions will need to be met to achieve this:

Speed brake lever in retracted position but ground spoilers not armed and either:

- One main gear on the ground
- Reverse selected on at least one engine

Speed brake lever is not in the retracted position, or Ground spoilers armed and:

- One main gear on the ground
- Both thrust levers at / below idle position

Pitch Control

- 2 Elevators and a trimmable horizontal stabiliser (THS) control pitch.
- Maximum deflection - 30° nose up / 17° nose down.
- ELAC 2 controls the elevators and horizontal stabiliser
- Green hydraulics power the left elevator
- Yellow hydraulics power the right elevator
- THS is powered by one of 3 electric motors

One of 3 electric motors controls the Stabiliser. Mechanical control of the THS is achieved through the trim wheel, providing the green or yellow hydraulics are working. Mechanical control has priority over electrical control.

The Elevators are controlled by two large servojacks which are electrically controlled. A servo jack has 3 modes of operation:

Active	Servo jack position is electronically controlled
Damping	Servo jack follows surface movement
Centering	Servo jack is retained in its neutral position using hydraulics

Yaw Control

- One Rudder controls yaw on the A320
- ELACs control the yaw orders for turn co-ordination and dampening yaw oscillations and then transmit these to the FACs
- Mechanical control is achieved through the rudder pedals in the flight deck.
- Maximum rudder travel gradually reduces as speed increases.
- When slats are extended, full rudder travel authority is available.
- Rudder trim is controlled by 2 electric motors.
- In manual flight, rudder trim can be applied using the RUD TRIM switch and reset to zero using the reset button.

Normal Law

Ground Mode

Direct relationship between the sidestick and the elevator deflection. Before takeoff, the pilots manually adjust the THS to adjust for CG. Above 75 kts on takeoff, maximum up elevator deflection is reduced from 30° to 20°.

Flight Mode

A load factor demand - the sidestick sets the elevator and THS to maintain a load factor proportional to sidestick deflection. The sidestick now controls the elevator, THS, ailerons, spoilers and rudder.

With the sidestick neutral and wings level, 1g is maintained in pitch.

Sidestick movement in the roll axis commands a given rate of roll.

Flare Mode

Passing 50 ft, the THS is frozen producing a direct stick - elevator relationship.

The system memorises the aircrafts attitude at 50 ft. Passing 30 ft the system reduces the pitch attitude to 2° nose down over 8 seconds.

This gives the aircraft a natural feel to flare for landing.

Load Factor Limitation	
Clean Configuration	+ 2.6g to -1g
Other Configurations	+ 2g to 0g

If the pilots encounter a situation such as CFIT where they need to pull hard on the sidestick, this will initially be limited to 2.6g with full sidestick deflection. If the situation remains, pilots can maintain this full aft stick position, upon which the high A of A protection will take over.

Load factor protection enables the pilots to make an initial reaction to a situation, without worrying about over-stressing the aircraft.

Pitch Attitude Protection		
Config 0-3	30° nose up	-15° nose down
Config full	25° nose up	-15° nose down

The FD bars will disappear from PFD's if the pitch attitude exceeds 25° up, or 13° down. The bars will only return when the pitch angle has returned to somewhere between 10° down and 22° up.

High nose up attitude = Rapid energy loss

Low nose down attitude = Rapid energy gain

Bank Angle Protection

The system maintains positive spiral static stability for bank angles above 33°. Releasing the sidestick above 33°, the aircraft automatically reduces to 33°. Full sidestick deflection is 67°.

If Angle of attack protection is active and full lateral deflection is held, the bank angle will not go beyond 45°.

If high speed protection is active and full lateral deflection is held, the bank angle will not go beyond 40°.

If the bank angle exceeds 45°, the AP disconnects and the FD bars disappear.

FD bars return when the bank angle decreases to less than 40°.

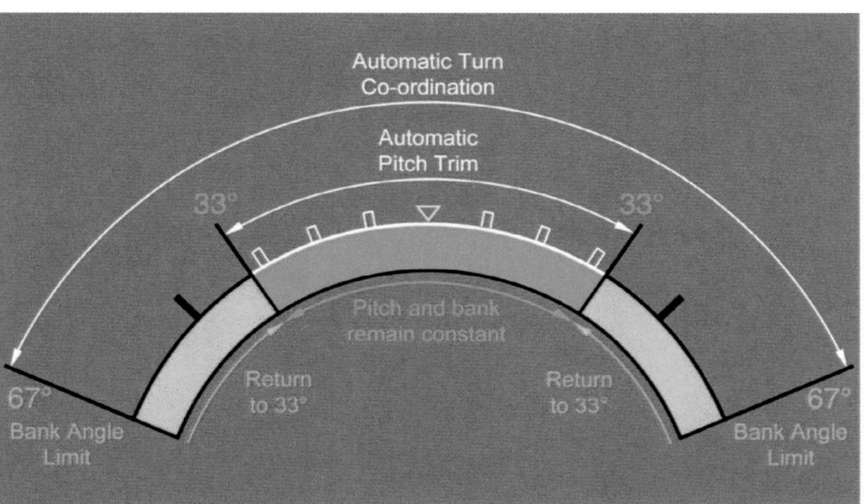

High Angle of Attack Protection

The aircraft is protected against stalling. When the angle of attack is greater that PROT, the angle of attack protection activates.

This protection has priority over all other protections.

The aircraft will maintain the angle of attack equal to PROT with no pilot input.

This can be increased by pilot input up to a maximum of MAX and when the sidestick is released, will return to PROT

When activated, sidestick input becomes an angle of attack demand, rather than a load factor demand.

PROT, Floor and MAX are computed based on the angle of attack, therefore will vary based on the aircrafts weight, configuration and load factor.

AP disconnects at PROT +1.

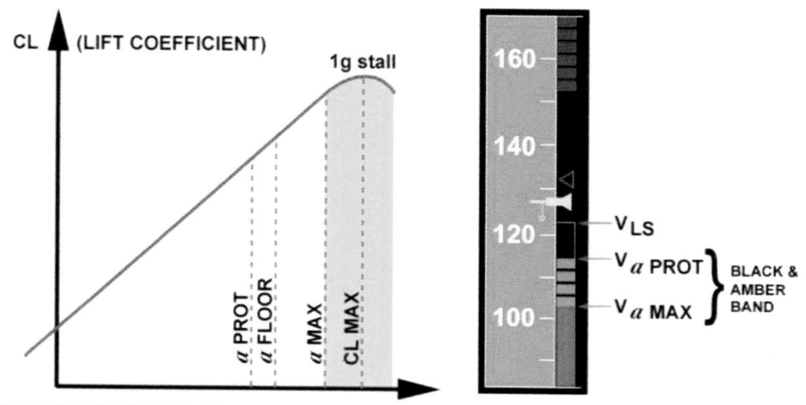

High Speed Protection

The A320 will automatically recover from a high speed condition.

If the speed increases above VMO/MMO, nose down authority is reduced and a nose up order is introduced.

A green ' = ' on the speed tape at VMO +6kts shows where the high speed protection starts.

The AP will disconnect when the high speed protection becomes active at VMO +6 kts.

Alpha Floor Protection

Alpha floor is an autothrust generated protection, not a flight control protection.

It is available from liftoff until 100 ft on landing. When the angle of attack becomes excessive, the FACs order TOGA thrust, regardless of the position of the thrust levers.

To get out of the alpha floor condition, the pilot must ensure the speed is safe to disconnect the autothrust. The thrust levers must be returned to the CLB gate and the A/THR pb on the FCU can then be engaged.

Alpha floor is activated when:	
α is greater than a floor:	
9.5°	Configuration 0
15°	Configuration 1 and 2
14°	Configuration 3
13°	Configuration FULL or sidestick greater than 14° nose up with A of A protection active

Alpha floor is lost when:	
One of the following failures:	SFCC 1 and FAC 2
	SFCC 2 and FAC 1
	Both FCU Channels
	1 EIU
	Both FMGC's
Alternate or Direct law	
Engine out when flaps / slats extended	
Engine failure with derated takeoff	

Alternate Law

Some failures on the aircraft can cause the flight control laws to downgrade.

- Pitch control is similar to normal law.
- Roll control is the same as direct law, with sidestick demanding aileron deflection rather than a roll rate.

Alternate Law Protections

Load factor limitation

The same as normal law, available with reduced protections and without reduced protections.

Pitch attitude protection

Not available in alternate law, the = symbols will be replaced by amber X symbols.

Bank angle protection

Not available in alternate law, the = symbols will be replaced by amber X symbols.

High speed protection

Changes to 'High speed stability' and is available with reduced protections.

Above VMO/MMO, a nose up demand is introduced to avoid excessive speed. The pilot can override this.

High angle of attack protection

Changes to 'Low speed stability' and is available only with reduced protections.

Low speed stability

Artificial low speed stability replaces angle of attack protection. This is active from 5-10 kts above the stall warning speed, depending on weight and configuration.

A gentle nose down order is introduced which will prevent the speed from going below VSW - stall warning speed.

Alpha floor protection is not available. Stalls can occur therefore stall recovery is the pilot's responsibility.

In alternate law, when the gear is selected down, the aircraft reverts to Direct Law.

Direct Law

As a result of some failures, the aircraft will revert to direct law once the landing gear is selected down. The sidestick inputs are now directly coupled to the controls. Manual pitch trim is used and no flight envelope protection is now available.

The aircraft will feel very sensitive in yaw and roll and whilst turning co-ordination is lost.

'USE MAN PITCH TRIM' will be displayed on the PFD in amber.

Mechanical Back-up

This is an extremely dangerous situation. Pitch trim and the rudder can be used to control the aircraft. THS will control the aircraft in pitch, rudder will be used to control the aircraft laterally.

'MAN PITCH TRIM ONLY' will be displayed on the PF

Flight Control Laws Summary

	NORMAL	ALTERNATE	DIRECT	MECH BACK-UP
PITCH	= LOAD FACTOR DEMAND ATTITUDE PROTECTION +30° (25°) to -15° =	×× LOAD FACTOR DEMAND NO ATTITUDE PROTECTION ××	USE MAN PITCH TRIM (PFD amber) DIRECT STICK TO ELEVATOR	MAN PITCH TRIM ONLY (PFD red) STABILIZER via PITCH TRIM WHEEL
ROLL	\\\\ // RATE OF ROLL UP TO 15° / SEC MAX BANK 67°	× × DIRECT STICK TO AILERONS + SP 4 & 5 UP TO 30° / SEC NO BANK LIMIT	DIRECT STICK TO AILERONS + SP 4 & 5 UP TO 30° / SEC NO BANK LIMIT	RUDDER
OVERSPEED	340 = 320 MMO/VMO PROTECTION	STABILITY ? OVERRIDE POSSIBLE	N/A	N/A
'G' FORCE	CLEAN: +2.5 to -1.0 G FLAP EXT: +2.0 to 0 G	CLEAN: +2.5 to -1.0 G FLAP EXT: +2.0 to 0 G	N/A	N/A
STALL	PROTECTION 160 140 VLS V∝ PROT ∝ FLOOR V∝ MAX	STABILITY ? O/RIDE POSSIBLE 160 140 VLS VSW	N/A	N/A

These 2 green lines indicate the aircraft is in Normal Law

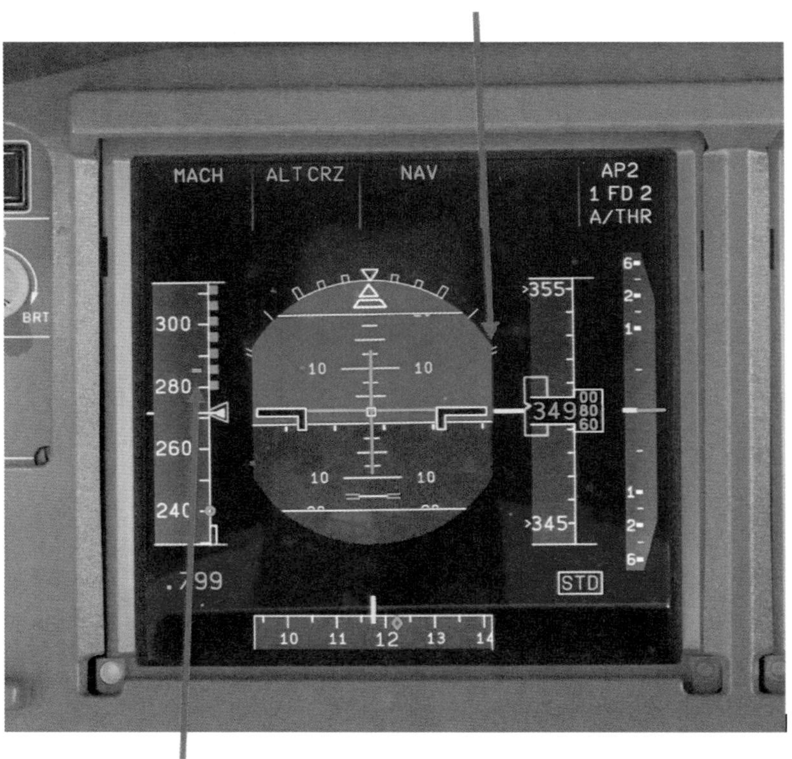

These 2 green lines indicate the start of High Speed Protection

Limitations	
Max altitude with slats/flaps extended	20,000 ft
Max operating speed	300 kts / M 0.82

Flap Position Limitations

Lever Position	Configuration	Max Speed	Flight Phase
0		VMO / MMO	Cruise
1	1	230 kts	Holding / App
	1 + F	215 Kts	Takeoff
2	2	200 Kts	Takeoff / App
3	3	185 Kts	App / Landing
FULL	4	177 Kts	Landing

Questions & Answers

Q. Which hydraulic systems actuate the ailerons?
A. Ailerons are hydraulically actuated by the jacks which are powered by the green and blue systems. One system works at a time, the green is the primary system.

Q. Which flight computers control the ailerons?
A. Controlled by ELAC 1. If ELAC 1 fails ELAC 2 takes over. If both ELAC's fail, the SEC's can provide roll via the spoilers.

Q. Which spoilers are used for ground lift dumping?
A. All 5 pairs of spoilers.

Q. Which spoilers are used for the speedbrakes?
A. Spoilers 2,3,4

Q. When will the spoilers automatically fully deploy during the landing phase?
A. Both main gears on the ground and the thrust levers at idle. If not armed, the spoilers deploy when reverse thrust is selected.

Q. If a spoiler is deployed and a hydraulic system fails, what happens?
A. The spoiler will maintain its last position at the time of the failure.

Q. How does the rudder travel limiter function?
A. At high speeds it prevents large rudder movements by restricting the rudder movement range, reducing excess strain on the fuselage. 2 motors control the rudder trim and artificial feel unit.

Q. If the rudder travel limiter fails in flight, what is the consequence?
A. The last setting will be maintained. When slats are extended, the travel limiter motors at low speed to allow full rudder deflection for approach and landing.

Q. What conditions cause speedbrake inhibition?
A. Config full TOGA AOA Protection Elevator Fault SEC 1 & 3 Fault

Q. What speed will the spoilers deploy in a rejected takeoff?
A. Above 72 kts

Q. What is phased lift dumping?
A. At touchdown with the thrust levers at idle and one main gear still airborne and one on the ground, spoilers partially deploy on the airborne side to force the wing and gear down.

Q. How many slats / flaps are there?
A. 5 leading edge slats, 2 trailing edge flaps

Q. If one of the hydraulic inputs or computers fail, what is the effect on flight controls?
A. They will travel at half speed

Q. If the sidestick is released at alpha max, what happens?
A. Attitude will return to alpha prot

Q. What does the AOA protection give protection against?
A. Stalling & windshear

Q. How do you recover if alpha floor activates?
A. Press the instinctive pb on the thrust levers. Move the thrust levers out of the CLB gate, or put them in the CLB gate and reinstate the ATHR using the FCU pb.

Q. If you press the instinctive pb on the thrust levers for more than 15s, what happens?
A. Autothrust is disengaged for the remainder of the flight. Alpha floor is not available.

Q. Does alpha floor work in alternate law?
A. No

Q. What is the load alleviation function?
A. An automatic function in normal law when in clean flight. Loads on the wing can be unloaded by inverting the ailerons and deploying spoilers.

Q. What is the max bank angle in normal law?
A. 67°

Q. What happens at max bank angle when the sidestick is released?
A. Aircraft returns to 33° angle of bank.

Q. Centering the beta target when single engine provides what?
A. Minimum drag / best climb performance.

Q. Max roll rate in normal law?
A. 15° per second

Q. What is the low energy warning?
A. Active below 2000 ft rad alt in config 2, 3 or full in normal law. It warns the pilots of a low energy situation developing before alpha prot and alpha floor are triggered, giving the pilots time to react. The audio calls 'SPEED SPEED SPEED' will be heard.

Q. When is the low energy warning inhibited?
A. Below 100 ft rad alt TOGA selected During an EGPWS alert Dual rad alt failure

Q. When is the low energy warning inhibited?

A. Below 100 ft rad alt

TOGA selected

During an EGPWS alert

Dual rad alt failure

Q. What is alpha lock and when does it activate?

A. Prevents slat retraction at high attitudes and low speeds and prevents low energy situations and stalls. Active below 148 kts and A of A greater than 8.5°. When activated, it remains active until the attitude is below 7.6° and speed has increased above 154 kts.

Q. In normal law, when will auto trim stop functioning?

A. When a manual input is made, rad alt below 50 ft, load factor below 0.5g and when some normal law protections are active.

Q. In normal law, when will auto trim stop functioning?

A. When a manual input is made, rad alt below 50 ft, load factor below 0.5g and when some normal law protections are active.

Q. What is the difference between alternate law with protections / without protections?

A. Alternate law with protections offers stabilities, mainly being high speed / low speed. These are not protections and they can be overridden by the pilot.

Q. What is Mechanical backup?
A. Results from the loss of all fly-by-wire computers. Is usually a temporary situation due to the loss of electrical power to the aircraft. Basic flying can be maintained using the THS and the rudder.

Q. What happens if a flap / slat deploys unevenly?
A. The wing tip brake will be deployed which will prevent any further movement. This can only be reset on the ground by an engineer.

Failures

F/CTL FLAPS / SLATS JAMMED

Threats	
Aviate, Navigate, Communicate	
Pull for speed as to not overspeed the current flap setting or decelerate below current speed limitation. Establish a max operating speed.	
Fuel burn will be greatly increased:	
Slats Extended:	Fuel burn increased by 60%
Flaps Extended:	Fuel burn increased by 80%

There are 2 scenarios with this fault which are:

- Flaps/slats locked with the wing tip brake on when selecting a different flap setting. In this situation, do not recycle the flap lever.
- Flaps/slats fail to move with flap lever movement - recycle the flap lever.

Initial ECAM is relatively straightforward however, thought needs to be given to landing distance required (as a worst case increased by x 2.2)

The flap / slat systems operate independently, the flap lever will still move the flaps even if the slats are locked and vice versa. Flap 3 should be used for landing.

The QRH must be consulted to establish what to do next. Landing distance and weather will determine a suitable airfield. A long final is advised to allow time to configure.

Approach & Landing	
SPEED SEL....................................VFE NEXT -5 kt The idea here is to slow the aircraft down enough to prevent an overspeed warning when selecting the next stage of flap, but not too slow as the actual flap/slat configuration will be less than what the S or F speed is normally based upon.	
Autopilot may be used down to 500 ft	CAT 1 approach only
Flap 3 Landing required	Landing Distance Calculation required
Characteristic speeds may be lost, in this case use the placard speeds to configure for each flap setting	
Use selected speed	
Overspeed and VLS are calculated depending on the actual slat/flap configuration.	
VFE/VFE next displayed are according to the flap lever position.	
If the stall warner activates, hold the speed to allow deployment of the flaps to recover the stall margin. A very gentle nose down demand on the sidestick can help reduce the A of A and thus stall warning activation at this point.	

Once in the landing configuration, the next thing to consider is the flare. As the pitch attitude will be greater than normal, ensure the flare is shallow as to avoid a tail strike.

If a go-around needs to be carried out, maintain the current flap/slat configuration. The QRH will advise on a max speed for the go around so ensure you brief this before the approach. Max speed -10 kts is advised.

Threats
Aviate, Navigate, Communicate
The ELAC's may not detect this fault, in this case normal law remains and there will be no ECAM warning.
QRH procedure to be applied if no ECAM
If ECAM procedure is shown, the aircraft reverts to alternate law.

At landing gear extension, the aircraft goes into direct law. The auto trim function is now lost therefore it is advisable to request a long final, establish VAPP, flap 3 then gear down. The mean elevator position will be memorised and becomes the reference for neutral sidestick.

Approach & Landing	
CAT 1 only	
It may be possible to use manual pitch trim, if available trim for neutral elevators.	
Gear Extension - Direct Law	Request Long Final
	VAPP, Flap 3, Gear Down

Whilst this may seem an issue, it is actually fairly easy to handle and a precautionary landing should follow.

F/CTL FLAP SYS 1/2 FAULT

Whilst this failure may at first appear to be a problem, thanks to redundancy of the system, the approach may be continued without any major issues.

If FLAP SYS 1 FAULT is shown - GPWS FLAP MODE - OFF

This is because the position of the flaps is not known to the GPWS system so prevents any unnecessary warnings on the approach.

Approach & Landing
ENG 1/2 APPR IDLE ONLY
FLAPS SLOW

The only issue here is that the flaps may run a little slower than normal. To mitigate a rushed approach, you may ask for a longer final approach to become stabilised earlier.

FUEL

Fuel is stored in the centre tank under the aircraft belly, and in the wings which have inner and outer tanks. There is a vent surge tank outboard of the outer tank in each wing. The outer tanks are used for wing bending and flutter relief.

Fuel can expand by 2% without spilling when the aircraft has been fueled to maximum capacity.

Each engine is supplied by one pump in the centre tank or two pumps in its own inner tank side.

There are 2 electrical transfer valves in each wing that allows fuel to transfer from outer to inner tanks - these are controlled by level sensors in the tanks. When any sensor detects the fuel quantity in an inner tank falling below 750 kg, it opens symmetrical transfer valves (one in each wing) allowing fuel in the outer tanks to transfer to the inner tanks. Once open, the valves remain open until refueling on the ground begins.

This process is indicated by the memo 'OUTER TK FUEL XFRD' and green triangles on the ECAM fuel page.

A cross feed valve allows both engines to be fed from one side or one engine to be fed from both sides.

To starve the engines of fuel the LP valves are closed. This is controlled by the following actions:

- ENG FIRE PB
- Engine master switch

The inner and outer tanks are connected via a spill pipe. This enables fuel returned to outer tanks via the recirculation system to flow into the inner tanks if the outer tanks are full. This is also used during the refueling process.

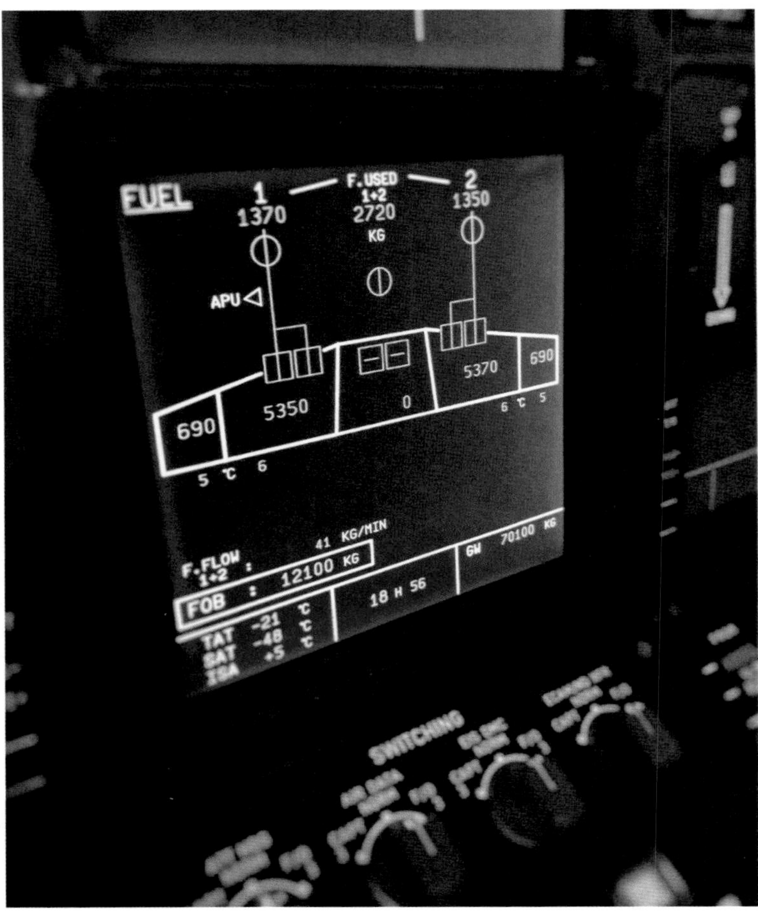

Fuel feed sequence

The inner tanks feed the fuel to the engines and empty in the following sequence:

- Centre tanks Fuel transfers to the inner tanks
- Inner tanks Tank empties down to 750 kg
- Outer tanks Fuel transfers into the inner tanks

The Fuel Level Sensing Control Unit (FLSCU) automatically controls the transfer valves. When the valves open, fuel from the inner tank pumps flow through the jet pump and create a suction in it. This suction then moves the fuel from the centre tank to the inner tanks. This allows for gravity fuel feeding should the pumps loose power.

In automatic mode, a pump is inhibited when the slats are extended, when a wing tank is full or after 5 minutes has passed since the centre tank reached low level. The exception to this is that 2 minutes after engine start, the pump is only inhibited by the centre tank low fuel condition.

When the inner tanks are full, the FLSCU closes the centre tank transfer valves. These are only re-opened when the engines have used 500 kg of the inner tank fuel.

Some fuel from each engine travels from the HP fuel line, via the IDG (to absorb heat), to the fuel return valve and then back to the outer tank. This results in IDG cooling when oil temperatures are high or when at low engine power.

If the outer tank is full, the fuel overflows via the spill pipe to the inner tank. Due to this recirculation process, the system automatically selects the CTR TK PUMP off when the inner tank is full. The wing tank pumps will feed until the engine has used 500 kg of fuel to ensure that no fuel is vented overboard.

Under each wing there is a fuel over pressure relief port with a detection disk. This ruptures if the internal and external pressure differential exceeds a predetermined level. Each relief port is secured closed by a black carbon disk. A white X indicates that the disk is intact and that the relief port is closed.

There is also a magnetic fuel level indicator under the wing allowing fuel to be measured manually. As well as water drain valves for each tank there is also a shroud drain under the fuselage to drain any fuel leaking from the system.

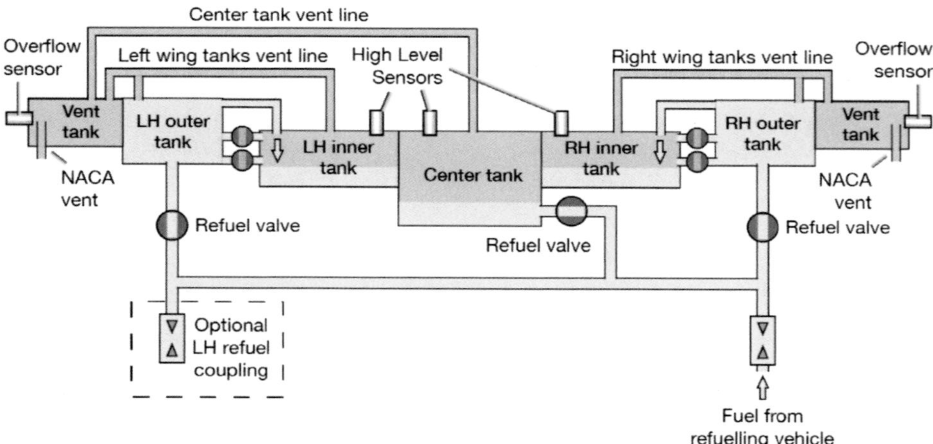

A319 / A320 without jet transfer pumps

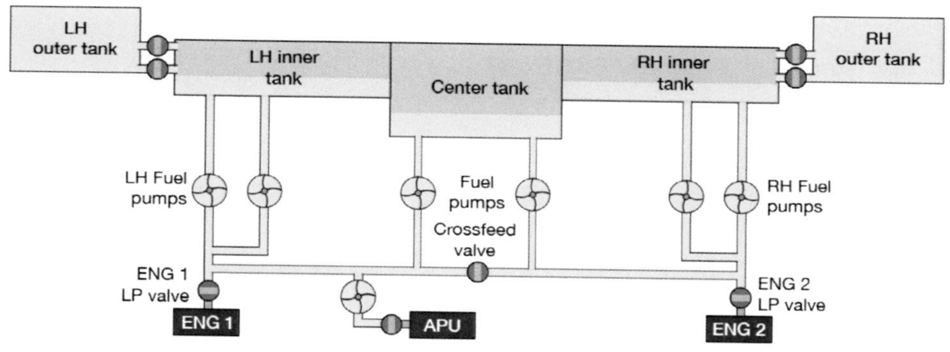

A319 / A320 / A321 with jet transfer pumps

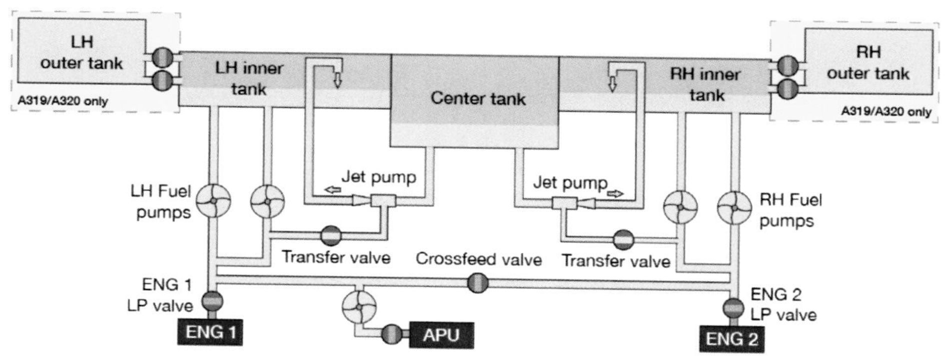

Limitations	
Minimum fuel temperature	-43°c
Maximum fuel temperature	54°c
Minimum fuel quantity at takeoff	1500 kg

Approximate fuel capacity A320 NEO				
	Lt	**USG**	**KG**	**Lb**
Outer Tanks x 2	864	228	678	1494
Inner Tanks x 2	6874	1816	5396	11896
Centre Tank	8248	2178	6474	14274
Total	23724	6267	18623	41054

Approximate fuel capacity A321 NEO				
	Lt	**USG**	**KG**	**Lb**
Wing Tanks x 2	7690	2032	6037	13311
Centre Tank	8200	2166	6437	14189
ACT (Additional Centre Tank)	2992	790	2348	5175
NO ACT	23580	6230	18511	40811
1 ACT	26572	7020	20859	45986
2 ACTs	29564	7810	23207	51161

Questions & Answers

Q. Which side supplies the APU with fuel?
A. The APU is supplied by engine No.1

Q. What are the suction valves?
A. The suction valves are held closed by fuel tank pressure created by the tank pumps. They are located in the inner tank. In an electrical failure, they remain open as the pressure within the tanks fails and the engines will be able to be gravity fed.

Q. Describe the fuel recirculating system
A. Fuel from the HP fuel valve is diverted through the heat exchanger of the IDG. Heat from the oil within the IDG is radiated through the fuel in the exchanger which in turn heats the fuel in the tanks. Fuel is then routed via the HP fuel feed and sent back to the outer tanks.

Q. How is centre tank fuel prioritised?
A. Centre tank fuel pumps deliver fuel at a higher pressure than the fuel pumps of the inner tanks. Because of this, when the centre tank pumps are on, the centre tank will drain before the inner tanks.

Q. Why is centre tank fuel prohibited for takeoff?
A. If the centre tank fuel was used during takeoff, any fuel returned to the outer tanks from the recirculating system would cause the tank surge vent to spill the excess fuel overboard.

Q. Can you refuel on battery power only?
A. Yes as there is a switch on the refueling panel to enable this to happen.

Q. What are fuel jet pumps?
A. There is 1 jet pump in each inner tank and the function is to draw fuel from the centre tank to the inner tank. This is done by creating a vacuum that pulls fuel through the centre tank transfer valves.

Failures

FUEL LEAK

Threats
Aviate, Navigate, Communicate
Consider potential divert options, expand range and view suitable airports.
Identify the source of the fuel leak by reference to the QRH and checking the Fuel SD page.
CM2 to fly the aircraft and CM1 to deal with the failure and ensure the aircraft is secure and fuel is preserved where possible.

This is a time critical failure and care must be taken to establish the source of the fuel leak. This could be either from the Centre tank, inner tanks or from the engine / pylon.

Leak confirmed from engine/pylon - Shut down engine to isolate fuel leak

Leak not confirmed - isolate each tank to check depletion rate from each tank.

Do not open the fuel X-feed unless you are absolutely sure that in doing so, all of your available fuel will not diminish. Use all available sources to confirm this including visual checks by cabin crew from the cabin windows, as well as the contents of the fuel tanks via the fuel SD page.

Approach & Landing	
LAND ASAP	MAYDAY Call
Avoid Holding	Use direct routing to an airport
Brief for single engine approach / landing / Go Around	
Do not use Reversers on landing	
Try to use full length of the runway to keep brake temperatures to a minimum.	

FUEL IMBALANCE

A fuel imbalance may occur for various reasons, the most common is with single engine operations and a fuel leak scenario.

Allow time for a fuel check to identify the correct tank if a fuel leak is suspected. If a fuel leak is suspected, refer immediately to the QRH FUEL LEAK procedure.

Whilst there is no mandatory need to balance the fuel tanks until the ECAM fuel advisory limit has been shown, it is considered good airmanship to balance the tanks at an appropriate time.

Advisory limit - One tank > 1500 kg than the other tank

Handling is not affected even with a maximum imbalance

To balance the fuel tanks:	
FUEL X FEED - ON	
On the lighter side and the centre tank:	FUEL PUMPS - OFF
When balanced:	FUEL PUMPS - ON
	FUEL X FEED - OFF

GRAVITY FUEL FEEDING

This procedure may be required if there is an issue with the fuel pumps.

- ENG MODE SEL - IGN

This protects the engine against any fuel interruptions

- Avoid Negative G Factor

Hopefully this will not be an issue as to keep gravity working in the correct direction.

There is an altitude restriction at which this procedure can be carried out. This is depending on weather the fuel has had time to deaerate or not.

FL360 if flight time above FL300 greater than 30 mins
FL260 if flight time above FL300 less than 30 mins
FL150 or 7000 ft above takeoff airport if FL300 never exceeded

When at gravity feed ceiling:

- FUEL X FEED - OFF

If no fuel leak and with one engine running:

- FUEL X FEED - ON
- BANK ANGLE - 1 DEGREE WING DOWN ON LIVE SIDE

This ensures fuel on the running engine side is used.

- RUDDER TRIM - USE

Use to maintain the correct course

If the imbalance reaches 1000 kg or more, adjust the wing bank angle to 2-3 degrees wing down.

HYDRAULICS

The A320 has 3 hydraulic systems, Green, Blue and Yellow. Each of these have individual reservoirs which are pressurised primarily by engine pumps, but if there is low pressure then bleed air can be used from the cross-bleed duct. Normal pressure is via the engine driven pumps and electric pump is 3000 psi.

The green and yellow hydraulic systems are pressurised by engine driven pumps. If the fire pb is pushed, a shutoff valve upstream will stop the flow of hydraulic pressure. The yellow system can also be pressurised by an electric pump which can be powered externally or via AC2. When the cargo doors are moved, this operates automatically and partially pressurises the system. This system can be selected on manually using the pb on the HYD overhead panel. Additionally, there is a hand pump to partially pressurise the system and open the cargo door in the event that no power is available.

The blue system is usually pressurised by an electric pump which is powered by AC1. When AC power is available the pump will operate - unless on the ground with both engines shut down. The above diagram shows the basics of the system pressurisation.

In abnormal situations, the blue hydraulic system can be pressurised by a Ram Air Turbine (RAT). This will deploy automatically should AC BUS 1 & 2 fail. In this case, the RAT cannot be restored in flight, only on the ground. The RAT will supply around 2500 psi. Activation can also be achieved through the RAT MAN ON pb.

To adapt for transient demands on the hydraulic systems and to maintain a constant pressure, each system has an accumulator fitted. If the pressure gets too low, a priority valve cuts off hydraulic supply to heavy users such as flaps / slats / gear and prioritises the primary flight controls.

When differential pressure between the Green and Yellow systems is greater than 500psi, a Power Transfer Unit (PTU) allows for cross pressurisation. The PTU activates automatically, however is inhibited when the first engine is started and during the second engine start sequence. It is also inhibited during and also for 40 s after operation of the yellow electric pump.

A320 Power Transfer Unit (PTU)

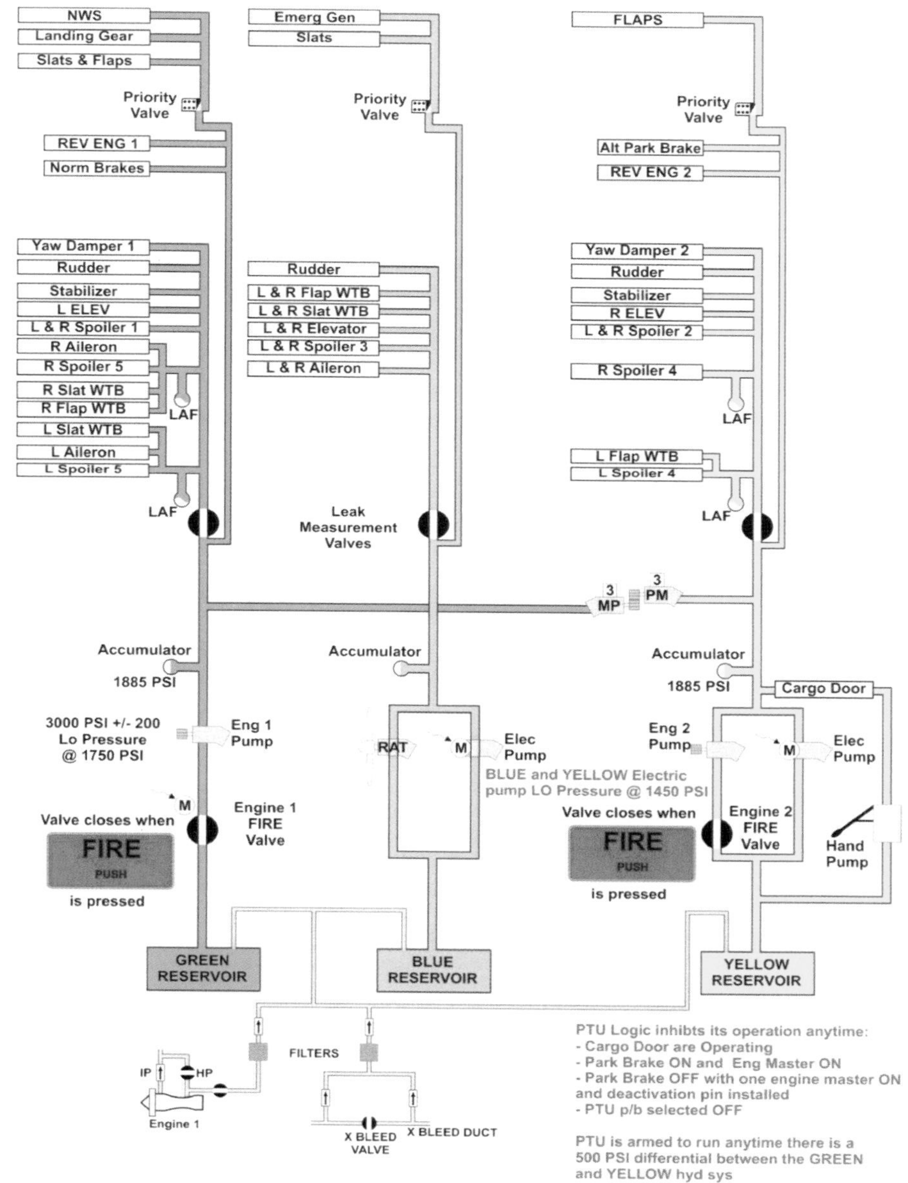

NWS
Landing Gear
Slats & Flaps
Priority Valve
REV ENG 1
Norm Brakes
Emerg Gen
Slats
Priority Valve
FLAPS
Priority Valve
Alt Park Brake
REV ENG 2
Yaw Damper 1
Rudder
Stabilizer
L ELEV
L & R Spoiler 1
R Aileron
R Spoiler 5
R Slat WTB
R Flap WTB
LAF
L Slat WTB
L Aileron
L Spoiler 5
LAF
Rudder
L & R Flap WTB
L & R Slat WTB
L & R Elevator
L & R Spoiler 3
L & R Aileron
Yaw Damper 2
Rudder
Stabilizer
R ELEV
L & R Spoiler 2
R Spoiler 4
LAF
L Flap WTB
L Spoiler 4
LAF
Leak Measurement Valves
3 MP
3 PM
Accumulator
1885 PSI
Accumulator
Accumulator
1885 PSI
Cargo Door
3000 PSI +/- 200
Lo Pressure
@ 1750 PSI
Eng 1 Pump
RAT
M
Elec Pump
BLUE and YELLOW Electric pump LO Pressure @ 1450 PSI
Eng 2 Pump
M
Elec Pump
M
Valve closes when
FIRE
PUSH
is pressed
Engine 1 FIRE Valve
Valve closes when
FIRE
PUSH
is pressed
Engine 2 FIRE Valve
Hand Pump
GREEN RESERVOIR
BLUE RESERVOIR
YELLOW RESERVOIR
FILTERS
IP
HP
Engine 1
X BLEED VALVE
X BLEED DUCT
PTU Logic inhibts its operation anytime:
- Cargo Door are Operating
- Park Brake ON and Eng Master ON
- Park Brake OFF with one engine master ON and deactivation pin installed
- PTU p/b selected OFF
PTU is armed to run anytime there is a 500 PSI differential between the GREEN and YELLOW hyd sys

Questions & Answers

Q. What are the hydraulic system pressure limitations?
A. 3000 +/- 200 psi

Q. How does the hydraulic system generate pressure?
A. The green system is powered by an engine driven pump or if needed by the PTU. The yellow system is pressurised by an engine driven pump or again by the PTU should an engine fail. An electric pump can pressurise the yellow system at any time, but mainly is used to allow for cargo door operation on the ground. The blue system is powered by an electric pump, or by the RAT following a pump failure.

Q. What is the hydraulic pressure with the RAT online?
A. 2500 psi

Q. What do the priority valves do?
A. Protect against low pressure. They cut off hydraulic power to heavy load users.

Q. How are the hydraulic reservoirs usually pressurised?
A. Bleed air from engine 1 usually pressurises the hydraulic reservoirs. If engine 1 fails or bleed air is too low, the system automatically takes the air from the crossbleed duct to prevent the pumps from cavitating.

Q. Which systems have fire shutoff valves?
A. Green and Yellow systems

Q. How does the PTU operate during engine start?
A. The PTU is inhibited during the first engine start, it then self tests at the beginning of the second engine start.

Q. What is the hydraulic accumulator?
A. A way of storing hydraulic pressure for use when no other means of hydraulic pressure is available. It also helps to maintain a constant pressure by covering transient demands during normal operation of the system. The yellow system accumulator will provide 7 full brake applications in the event of a system failure. The accumulator can be recharged by using the yellow electric pump.

Q. What do the red guarded switches have in common?
A. The actions of pressing them is irreversible.

Failures

Failure of a single hydraulic system will not be too much of a problem due to the redundancy of other systems that can take up the slack. The aircraft will revert to CAT 3 Single.

If 2 hydraulic systems are lost, then this can prove to be a little more of a problem. There are many things to consider before a safe landing can be carried out such as:

- Landing in abnormal configuration
- Longer landing distance required
- Loss of autopilot
- Long ECAM / QRH procedures
- Aircraft handling characteristics

As the AP will disconnect, one pilot will fly the aircraft and the other will manage the checklists and prepare to configure for landing. This situation is a LAND ASAP, however the approach should only be commenced once both pilots are fully briefed and prepared.

Initial actions should be in a similar order to the below:

- FD off, TRK/FPA on - Fly the Aircraft
- ECAM Actions
- Status Page
- Option generation - decide on a landing airport.
- Brief the Approach and set up aircraft in the correct configuration.

BLUE Hydraulic Failure		
Procedure	**Affected Systems**	
SLATS SLOW	Flight Controls	Spoilers 3
Landing Distance Procedure - Apply		Aileron R1, L2
		Elevator R1, L2
		SFCC 1 Slats
	Emergency Generator	

GREEN Hydraulic Failure		
Procedure	**Affected Systems**	
FLAPS SLOW	FLIGHT CONTROLS	Spoilers 1 + 5
SLATS SLOW		Inner Flaps
Landing Distance Procedure - Apply (Due to partial loss of spoilers)		Elevator 2
		Aileron R2, L1
		THS motor 1
		SFCC 1 Flaps
		SFCC 2 Slats
		Yaw Damper 1
	NW Steering	
L/G Gravity Extension	L/G Retraction	
After Landing, ask to be towed from runway	Normal & Auto brake	
	Reverser 1	

YELLOW Hydraulic Failure		
Procedure	**Affected Systems**	
FLAPS SLOW	FLIGHT CONTROLS	Spoilers 2 + 4
Landing Distance Procedure - Apply (Due to partial loss of spoilers)		Outer Flaps
		Elevator 3
		THS Motor 2
		SFCC Flaps
		Yaw Damper
	ANTI SKID	
	ALT & Park Brake	
	Reverser 2	

Green & Yellow Failure	
THS is stuck	
ELAC position Elevator to maintain G demand with sidestick center until L/G down	
To ensure full side stick authority for landing, pilots must stabilise at VAPP and landing configuration before L/G down	
Disregard - 'USE MANUAL PITCH TRIM'	
A/P inop	A/P 1+2 inop
AUTOTHRUST Available	ALTERNATE LAW Protection lost
SPEED select	• THS Stuck • SLATS SLOW • FLAPS INOP • SPOILERS 1,2,3,4 GND
LANDING - FLAP 3 'ON'	
GPWS FLAP MODE - OFF	
VAPP = Vref +25 (MCDU CONF3)	
L/G = GRAVITY EXTN	DIRECT LAW at Gear Down
Use QRH / Performance software to calculate LANDING DISTANCE	• L/G Retraction • ANTI-SKID • N/W STRNG
Braking - Y accumulator only. Max pressure 1000 psi	NORMAL & AUTOBRAKE inop REVERSE 1 + 2 inop

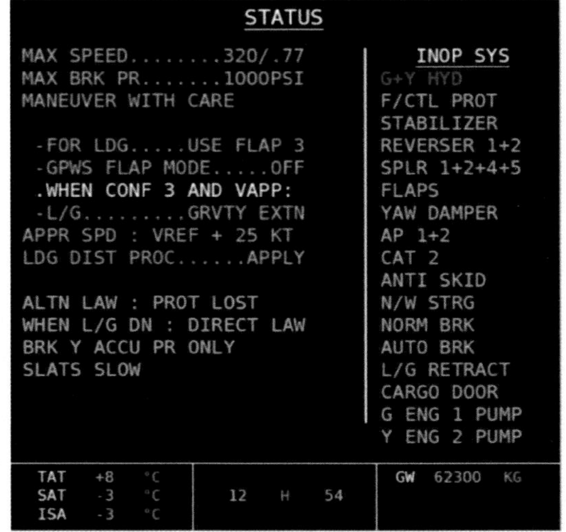

The key consideration here is the stopping distance due to loss of some spoilers, no reversers and Y accumulator pressure only. An airport with a long runway is preferential.

Approach
Alternate Law
CAT 1 only - 200 ft / 550 m
Use Flap 3 for landing
Flap Extension - VFE next -5 kts
Slats slow, flaps jammed
Establish calculated VAPP speed
L/G Gravity Extension
Flap 1, 2, 3, Vapp, Gear Down

Landing
Direct Law when gear down - handling may feel different
Only 1 spoiler per wing
No reversers available
Y accumulator pressure only for braking - 7 applications max
No nose-wheel steering - tug required to vacate runway

Go Around
L/G retraction unavailable

Green & Blue Failure	
RAT available for HYD pressure	
AUTO THRUST - OFF	
Only 1 Elevator surface	
No Ailerons & Slats	
L/G Gravity EXTN at 200 kts	
SPEED BRAKE- Do not use	
SPEED Select	A/P 1 + 2
Landing - USE FLAP 3	AUTO THRUST Disconnect
GPWS LDG FLAP 3 - ON	ALT LAW - Protection Lost
L/G GRAVITY EXTN at 200 kts No Slats for landing Use QRH / Performance software to calculate LANDING DISTANCE	• ELAC 1 INOP • Ailerons 1 + 2 • Spoilers inhibited • L Elevator failure • SLATS Slow • FLAPS Slow
Braking - Alternate + ANTI SKID	• L/G Down - DIRECT LAW • No N/W STRG • No L/G Retraction • EMERGENCY GENERATOR • Reverser 1 inop

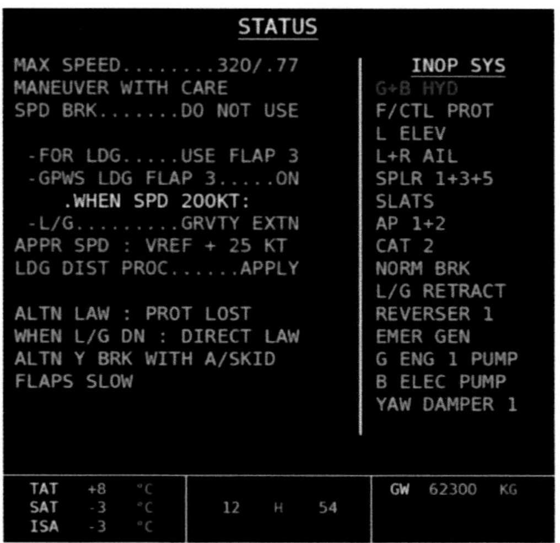

This failure requires careful handling of the aircraft due to the loss of Ailerons and only one Elevator available. To make maximum use of the remaining elevator, the gear is extended at 200 kts to revert to Direct Law sooner. A shorter runway may be acceptable but ideally without a strong crosswind.

Approach
Alternate Law
CAT 1 only - 200 ft / 550 m
Use Flap 3 for landing
Flap extension - VFE next -5kts
Slats jammed, flaps slow
When 200kts, L/G Gravity extension (Take care when flaps extend, may require downwards pitch) *Extending the L/G at 200 kts reverts to Direct Law sooner. This provides better pitch control than alternate law with 1 elevator and all slats lost.*
Decelerate to calculated VAPP
Flap 1, Gear Down, 2, 3, Vapp

Landing
Direct Law when gear down - handling may feel different
2 Spoilers per wing
REV 2 available only
Alternate braking available

Go Around
L/G retraction unavailable

Yellow & Blue Failure	
NORMAL Law	
L/G Gravity EXTN	
Landing - Config Full	
AUTOTHRUST - Available	AP 1 + 2 INOP
NORMAL Law	• R Elevator INOP • SLATS SLOW • FLAPS SLOW • Spoilers 2, 3, 4 • SPEED BRAKE
Use QRH / Performance software to calculate LANDING DISTANCE	REVERSER 2
Braking - NORMAL	EMERGENCY GENERATOR

```
STATUS

MAX SPEED........320/.77
MANEUVER WITH CARE
SPD BRK.......DO NOT USE

 .IF HYD NOT RECOVERED:
 -L/G.........GRVTY EXTN
LDG DIST PROC......APPLY

SLATS/FLAPS SLOW

INOP SYS
B+Y HYD
R ELEV
SPLR 2+3+4
SPD BRK
AP 1+2
CAT 2
N/W STRG
REVERSER 2
CARGO DOOR
EMER GEN
Y ENG 2 PUMP
B ELEC PUMP
YAW DAMPER 2

TAT +8 °C
SAT -3 °C
ISA -3 °C
12 H 54
GW 62300 KG
```

This failure is considered the most manageable of all 3 dual hydraulic failures. AP disconnects however the aircraft remains in Normal Law.

Approach
Normal Law
CAT 1 only - 200 ft / 550 m
Slats slow, Flaps slow
L/G Gravity Extension

Landing
2 Spoilers per wing
REV 1 available only
Normal braking available
No nose-wheel steering - tug required to vacate runway

Go Around
L/G retraction unavailable

ICE & RAIN

Engine Anti Ice

Each engines air intake is anti-iced using hot air from an independent bleed from the HP compressor. These are controlled using the ENG 1 and ENG 2 pb's on the overhead panel. If electrical power is lost, the valves fail in the open position. If no air is available, then the valves close.

If the TAT is 10°c or less and there is visible moisture, the Engine anti ice pb's should be selected ON. Standard temperature range is -40°c to +10°c

Wing Anti Ice

On each wing, 3 outboard slats are anti-iced using hot air from the pneumatic system. APU Bleed air must not be used for anti-icing due to a lack of temperature control of the air which could damage the slats. Each wing has a single electrical valve that controls the flow of air to the slats via the DC ESS SHED. Both of these valves are controlled via a single pb on the overhead panel.

If a leak is detected, the valve will automatically close on the affected side. This can cause a problem due to asymmetric icing which could form on the wing. On the ground, when the pb is selected on the system will perform a self-test for 30 seconds. If left selected on, the valves will open once airborne.

A320 / A321 NEO Anti Ice System

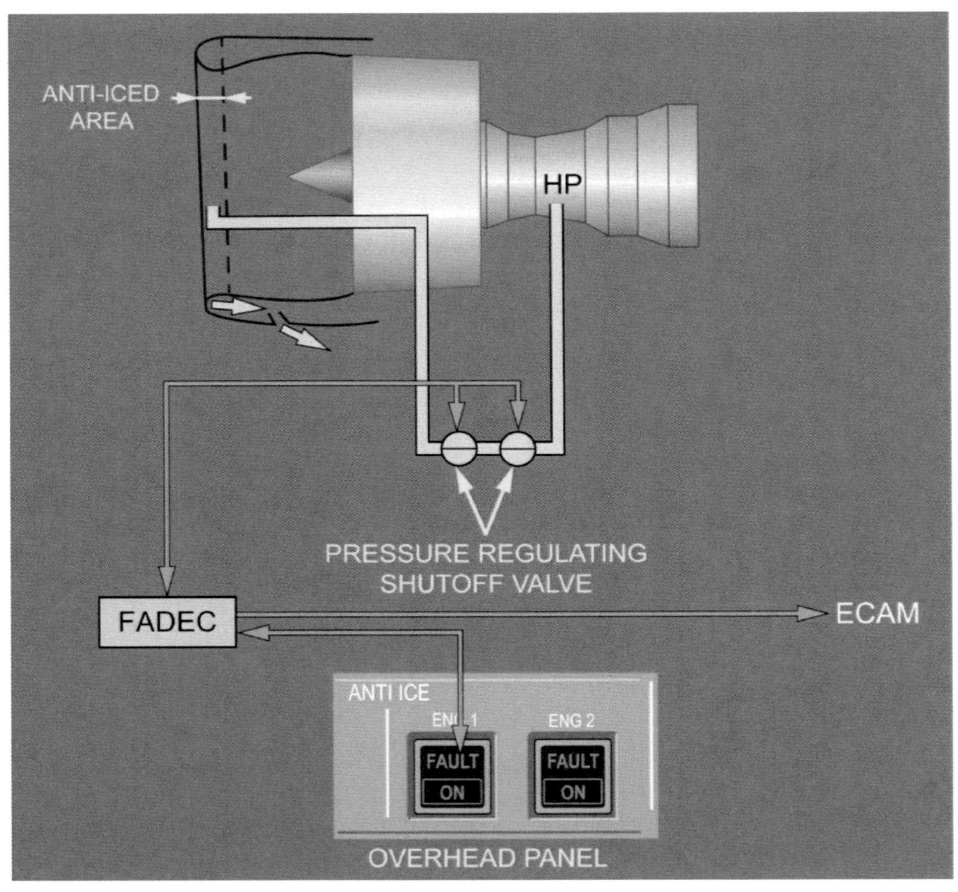

Window Heat

Both side windows and also the windscreen is heated electrically. This operates whenever at least one engine is running and whilst on the ground operates at a lower heat than when airborne. This is controlled using the PROBE/WINDOW HEAT pb on the overhead panel.

Probe Heat

Electrical heating is provided to the pitot heads, static heads, AofA probes, and TAT probes. There is a different Probe Heat Computer for the Captains, First Officers and standby probes which provides automatic regulation, fault detection and also overheat protection to each.

Rain Protection

In heavy rain, each windshield has a rain repellent which can be applied which should disperse the water allowing greater vision. This should only be used when airborne. The liquid is stored in a pressurised bottle in the cockpit and may produce a smell of orange peels if leaking.

Each windshield also has a wiper blade which can be used via a rotary selector on the overhead panel. This should only be used when 230 kt or less.

Water drain masts are heated to prevent ice formation. This heat is reduced whilst on the ground.

Q. What is the definition of icing conditions?
A. Icing Conditions are said to exist when the OAT on the ground or the TAT in flight is 10°C or less and visible moisture is present, such as clouds or fog, rain, snow, sleet or ice crystals or standing water, slush, ice or snow.

Q. What affect does using the engine anti-ice have on engine performance?
A. It reduces performance as bleed air is used for anti-icing purposes.

Q. After landing, if icing conditions are still present, when should the anti-ice pb be switched off?
A. Once safely parked on stand.

Q. On approach, when should the wing anti-ice be switched off?
A. Generally at around the FAF, however if the ice accretion is still visible then it can be left on until after landing,

Q. After takeoff, if wing anti-ice is needed, when should it be switched on?
A. After thrust reduction altitude

Q. Which slats are anti-iced?
A. The three outboard slats 3-4-5 of each wing are anti-iced

Q. When are the drain masts heated?
A. Any time there is electrical power to the aircraft they are heated.

Q. When will the probe heating come on?
A. When there is at least one engine running, and when the aircraft is in flight.

Q. Can the rain repellant be used on the ground?
A. No, it is inhibited on the ground.

LANDING GEAR

The landing gear is controlled by two Landing Gear Control and Interface Units (LGCIU). Each gear cycle is controlled by one LGCIU which then switches to the other once complete. Landing gear actuation is via the Green hydraulic system and a safety valve protects gear operation above 260 kts.

The gear can be operated in an emergency via a crank turning handle in the cockpit. This activates the safety valve which allows the gear to drop using gravity, however the gear doors will remain open.

The position of the landing gear is established using proximity detectors which are located on the following:

- Gear locks
- Gear doors
- Cargo doors
- Flaps
- Shock absorber struts

The gear fully locked down and in position is indicated on the ECAM as green triangles, 2 on each gear to indicate the two LGCIU's. The triangles are red when the gear is unlocked and show no colour once the gear is fully retracted.

Nose-wheel Steering

This is controlled by a 2 channel Brake and Steering Control Unit (BSCU) and actuated via the yellow hydraulic system. Up-to 20 kts, the steering hand-wheel has authority up-to 75° which reduces to 0 above 80 kts. When neither engines are running the steering servo valve is deactivated, allowing the nose-wheel to be moved up-to 95°.

Braking

There are 2 braking systems on the A320, the Normal system using the green hydraulics and the Alternate system using the Yellow system. This alternate system is backed up by an accumulator which has the potential to deliver 7 full brake applications in an emergency, and also provides parking brake pressure for just over 12 hours.

The BSCU provides the following:

- Wheel speed monitoring
- Antiskid
- Brake temperature monitoring
- Residual pressure check

During retraction of the gear, the main gear is automatically braked to slow wheel speed. The nose gear is braked by a brake band on older msn's.

Antiskid

The antiskid system measures the slip of the wheels similar to that used in cars. When the speed of the tyre reduces to around 0.87 of the aircraft speed, a servo valve releases the brakes. This system is unavailable with loss of BSCU and with Green and Yellow hydraulic system loss. It can also be manually switched off using the ASKID & NW STRG toggle switch.

Autobrake

Allows automatic deceleration of the aircraft at a given rate. This is available with the Normal braking system only. Autobrake activation is linked to the ground spoilers and hence will not activate below 72kts when the spoilers automatically operate on a rejected takeoff.

LO	4 seconds after ground spoiler extension - decelerates at 2 m/s
MED	2 seconds after ground spoiler extension - decelerates at 3 m/s
MAX	Maximum brake as soon as ground spoilers are extended

A green decal light indicates an 80% deceleration rate.

Autobrake is deactivated by pressing the brake pedals or pushing the autobrake pb.

Wheel temperature

Above 100°c	A green arc appears on the wheel SD page
Above 300°c	An amber arc appears on the wheel SD page

If brake fans are on, the temperature sensor cannot be accurate thus takeoff must be delayed until the temperature reaches 150°c.

If brake fans are off, brake temperature must not exceed 300°c prior to takeoff.

Limitations		
Maximum brake temperature for departure	150°c If brake fans used	
	300°c if no brake fans used	
°Max speed gear extended	280 kt	
Max speed gear extension	250 kt	
Max speed gear retraction	220 kt	
Max Tyre Speed	195 kt	
Max nosewheel steering angle	85° degrees	
Max Taxi Speed with deflated tyres	1 tyre per gear	7 kt
	2 tyres per gear	3 kt
	Max nosewheel steering	30°

Questions & Answers

Q. Which hydraulic system powers the nose-wheel steering?
A. Yellow system

Q. Above what speed is the steering tiller disabled?
A. Above 80 kts

Q. What happens if both steering tillers are moved at the same time?
A. Movements are added together and the result applied to the NWS

Q. What are the different types of braking available?	
A.	Normal brakes with anti-skid - Green Hydraulics Alternate brakes with anti-skid - Yellow Hydraulics Alternate brakes only - Yellow Hydraulics Hydraulic accumulator only

Q. What speed does the rudder disconnect from the NWS?
A. 130 kts.

Q. How many full braking applications are provided by accumulator braking?
A. 7 applications

Q. When does MAX autobrake function?
A. When thrust levers are closed and speed at least 72 kts

Q. When will the DECEL light illuminate during the landing roll?
A. When braking reaches 80% of the selected rate

Q. How does anti-skid function?
A. Wheel speed is maintained to the point just above an impending skid. Disabled below 20 kts.

Q. What is the tyre limiting speed?
A. 195 kts

Brake wear indicator

Failures

Landing with Abnormal Gear

If at least one green triangle is showing in each gear on the SD page, this confirms that the gear is down and locked. If this is not the case, the Abnormal gear checklist must be completed.

Nose Gear fault - Move CG aft by moving passengers to the rear of the aircraft. Lower the nose wheel gently onto the runway. Engines should be shut down prior to nose impact.

Main gear fault - Consider cross-feeding fuel to remove from the affected wing. Switch off the Anti-skid system to prevent permanent brake release. The ground spoilers should not be armed to maintain roll authority. At touchdown, engines to be shut down and affected wing to be kept from impact as long as possible.

Approach	
L/G Lever	Check Down
GRVTY GEAR EXTN handle	Turn back to normal - Reduces the chance of gear collapse on landing
No AUTOBRAKE	Autobrake cannot be activated with a landing gear in abnormal position. Manual braking provides better roll / pitch control
A/SKID & N/W STRG	OFF - Reference speed used for antiskid functions cannot be used. Turn OFF to prevent permanent brake release.
Max Brake 1000 psi	Due to no A/SKID available
If one or both MAIN L/G abnormal:	Do not arm Spoilers - Maintain roll control. Spoiler extension prevents spoilers acting as roll surfaces.

Touchdown	
Engines to be shut down early so fuel is shut off before impact of nacelles but late enough to maintain control via flight controls and Hydraulics.	
If NOSE L/G abnormal:	Keep Nose Up
	Brakes - Apply smoothly
	Before impact - ENG MASTERS OFF
If one MAIN L/G abnormal:	Touchdown - All ENG MASTERS OFF
	Affected side - Wing up
If both MAIN L/G abnormal	Flare - ALL ENG MASTERS OFF
	Min Pitch attitude - 6°

Hydraulic power will remain available for around 30s after engine shutdown.

Aircraft Stopped	
Park Brake	ON
ALL FIRE PB (ENG + APU)	PUSH
ALL AGENT (ENG + APU)	DISCH
If evacuation is required	Initiate
	Press EVAC COMMAND pb
If evacuation not required	Make PA to crew and passengers

Loss of Braking

This Memory Item requires immediate actions to be taken:

Reverser	MAX
Brake Pedals	Release
A/SKID & N/W STRG	OFF
Brake Pedals	Press
Max brake pressure	1000 psi

These actions should ensure the Alternate braking system comes into action. If this fails also then short applications of the parking brake should be used.

Care must be taken to maintain lateral control of the aircraft so delay this if possible until lower speeds.

Gear Not Up-locked

Recycle the gear if the retraction sequence has not finished after 30s. If this does not work, a return to the airport or a diversion must be initiated. If the gear doors are open due to the gear not fully retracted, then a fuel penalty may occur.

Gear Not Down-locked

If the gear extension has not completed after 30s, retract the gear and then re-deploy it. If this does not work, then apply the gravity gear extension checklist.

Landing Gear Gravity Extension

This is a relatively simple procedure and used for various system failures to preserve the hydraulic pressure that is required when the landing gear is extended.

GRAVITY GEAR EXTN Handcrank	PULL AND TURN *Rotate clockwise 3 times until the mechanical stop*
L/G Lever	DOWN
GEAR DOWN Indications	CHECK
The L/G LGCIU 2 FAULT or BRAKES SYS 1(2) FAULT alert may be spuriously triggered after gravity extension If the 3 green downlock arrows are not on, the handcrank may not be at the mechanical stop.	
If Successful	Do not reset the Gravity Gear Extn handcrank
If Unsuccessful	LDG WITH ABNORMAL L/G PROC - Apply

LIGHTS

The A320 has the following exterior lights:

- Navigation & Logo lights
- Landing lights
- Runway turn-off lights
- Takeoff / Taxi lights
- Anti-collision lights
- Strobe lights
- Wing / Engine scan lights

There is a single navigation light, Red on the left wing, Green on the right wing. There is also a white light on the APU tail cone. Below each navigation light is a small blue light which indicates the wear of the navigation lights. If this flashes, the lights should be replaced.

The logo lights are based on the upper surface of the horizontal stabiliser. They operate when the main landing gear is compressed and on some models when the flaps or slats are extended.

Landing lights can be selected to ON which extends and illuminates the lights. OFF turns the lights off however they remain extended. Retract turns off the lights and retracts the lights.

Runway turn-off lights are switched off automatically once the landing gear is retracted.

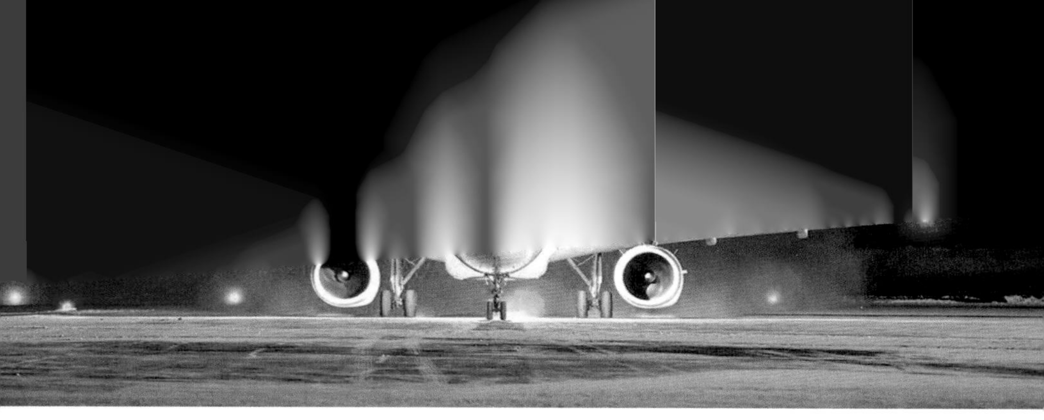

Takeoff / Taxi lights – TO illuminates both taxi and takeoff lights. Taxi only illuminates the taxi light. Both lights are on the nose gear and are automatically turned off at gear retraction.

The anti-collision or Beacon light is located on the upper and lower fuselage and flashes a red light to indicate engines are running.

Strobe lights are located on each wing and below the tail cone and flash in synchronisation. ON turns all lights on. AUTO turns the lights on automatically when the main gear is not compressed.

Wing lights are located on both sides of the fuselage forward of the leading edge of the wing. They illuminate the wing leading edge and engines to visually detect any possible ice accretion.

Landing Light in retracted position

Interior Lights

The Dome light is the only light with battery protection and due to this, DIM is the recommended position for takeoff.

Seatbelt and No smoking signs have 3 positions:

ON	Signs on in the cabin
AUTO	Signs on when gear is extended or flaps/slats extended
OFF	Signs off in the cabin

Emergency lights consist of the following:

- Proximity emergency escape path marking
- Overhead emergency lights
- EXIT signs
- Lavatory auxiliary lights
- Overwing escape lighting
- Escape slide lighting

Exit markers are located next to each emergency exit door at the front, rear and middle of the cabin.

Exit signs are located in bright white above each emergency exit door.

Floor lighting illuminates the emergency escape path for passengers to follow.

Internal batteries supply power to the escape paths and exit markers. These batteries are independent to the main batteries and last for approximately 12 minutes.

The lavatory auxiliary lights will always remain on.

When the slides are armed and a door or emergency exit is opened, the escape slides integral lighting illuminates. These are supplied by internal batteries.

EMER EXIT LT Toggle Switch	
ON	Overhead emergency lights, EXIT signs and proximity marking system illuminates
OFF	The above lights are all off
ARM	Exit markers come on when electrical power is lost

Overhead emergency lights come on if normal electrical power fails, DC SHED ESS BUS fails, AC BUS 1 fails.

Exit signs come on if electrical power is lost or DC SHED ESS BUS fails.

Questions & Answers

Q. Is there a speed restriction to operate the landing lights?
A. No

Q. When do the strobe lights come on automatically?
A. When the toggle switch is in the AUTO position and the landing gear is not compressed.

Q. Do the RWY turnoff lights turn off automatically?
A. Yes, they automatically turn off once the landing gear is retracted

Q. What are the different Area Call Panel (ACP) lights shown in the cabin?	
A steady light is normal, a flashing light is an emergency call	
BLUE	Passenger call from the cabin with single chime
AMBER	Passenger call from the toilet with single chime
PINK	Cabin Crew to Cabin Crew call PILOTS to CABIN CREW call Associated with a high-low chime in cabin

Q. How long do the batteries last for emergency lighting?
A. 12 minutes

NAVIGATION

Navigation is provided by the aircrafts 3 Air Data Inertial Reference Units - ADIRS. ADIRU 1 & 2 are generally used by both pilots for data and the 3rd system is used as a backup or spare.

The system is split between two parts. The Air Data Reference computer and a laser gyro inertial reference system.

The ADR gathers data from the sensors and probes and computes data on the following:

- Angle of attack
- Temperature
- Altitude
- Airspeed / Mach number
- Overspeed warnings

The IR part of the system supplies data on the following:

- Heading
- Track
- Attitude
- Acceleration
- Ground speed
- Position
- Flight path vector

There are 4 different types of sensors and probes:

- Pitot probes - 3
- Static pressure probes - 6
- Angle of attack sensors - 3
- Total air temperature probes - 2

The A320 also uses 2 independent GPS receivers, which use 24 satellites to get an accurate position report. This information is then transferred to the ADIRS units, which is used to calculate its exact position. The FMGC's then use this information to allow us to enter our flight and route information.

When powering up the aircraft, the rotary selectors are turned to NAV which will align all 3 systems to ensure maximum accuracy of navigation. Alignment can take around 10 minutes and the ALIGN white light will illuminate throughout the process until complete.

Sometimes after a flight, the IR's need to be re-aligned if there is an inaccuracy. This is done by selecting the rotary selectors to OFF, then back to NAV within 5 seconds.

There is a backup compass and also an Integrated Standby Instrument System (ISIS) as a navigation backup.

Radio Navigation

AUTOMATIC	In normal operation, each FMGC will tune its own receiver
MANUAL	THE MCDU can be used to tune a specific navaid. This will be sent to both FMGC's, or onside in the case of a failure.
BACK-UP	If both FMGC's fail, navaids can still be tuned using the Radio Management Panel (RMP)

The aircraft has:

2 VOR receivers

2 ILS receivers

2 ADF

2 DME

Radio Altimeter

There are 2 radio altimeters on board, these work by timing how long it takes radio waves to reflect to the ground and back to the aircraft to give an accurate altitude reading. The radio height shows below 2500ft.

The CAPT PFD displays RA 1 height

The FO PFD displays RA 2 height

If one RA fails, both of the displays will show the height from the remaining RA.

Antenna & Probe locations

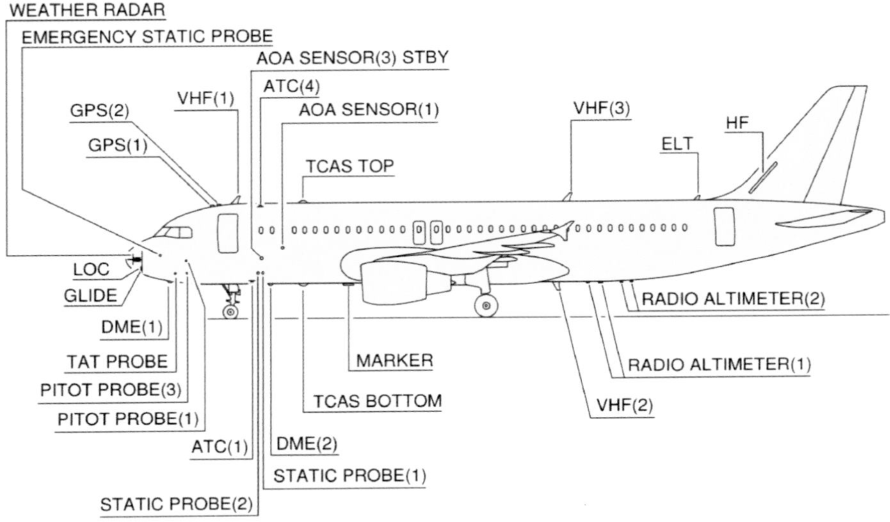

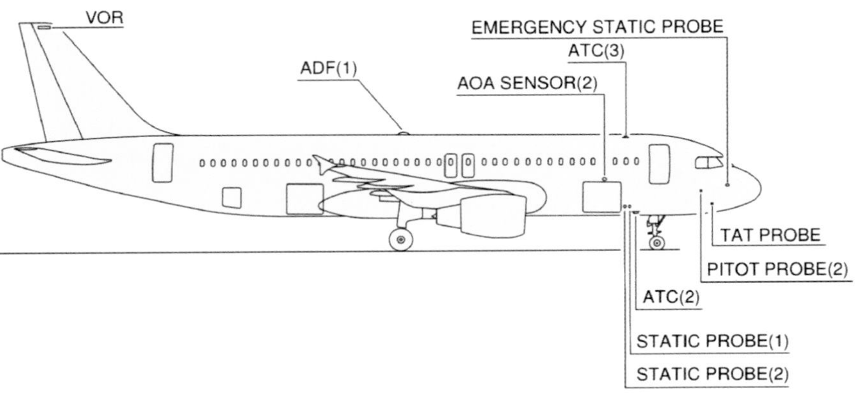

EGPWS

The Ground Proximity Warning System operates between 2450ft - 30ft and computes the aircraft altitude using the following:

- Pressure altitude
- Temperature
- GPS altitude
- Radio altitude
- Barometric reference

Its purpose is to warn the crew to imminent danger and proximity to terrain.

A Predicative GPWS system is used to display terrain information based on a GPWS database. This can be supplied by:

- Enhanced GPWS (EGPWS) by Honeywell
- ACSS (Aviation Communication & Surveillance Systems)
- GCAS (Ground Collision Avoidance System) via T2CAS / T3CAS

Predictive GPWS operates using the following:

- Obstacle database
- Forward looking terrain alerting function

To enable the pilots to see this terrain data, the brightness is controlled using the ND brightness knob and is then shown on the ND. This should always be turned up to max to enable pilots to view weather from the weather radar, as well as terrain.

<table>
<tr><td colspan="4">MODE 1 - Excessive rate of descent</td></tr>
<tr><td colspan="4">Based on radio height and rate of descent of the aircraft</td></tr>
<tr><td>CAUTION</td><td colspan="3">'SINK RATE, SINK RATE'</td></tr>
<tr><td>WARNING</td><td colspan="3">'PULL UP'</td></tr>
<tr><td colspan="4"></td></tr>
<tr><td colspan="4">MODE 2 - Excessive terrain closure rate</td></tr>
<tr><td colspan="4">Based on Gear, Flap / Slat configuration, RA and the RA rate of change</td></tr>
<tr><td>CAUTION</td><td colspan="3">'TERRAIN, TERRAIN'</td></tr>
<tr><td rowspan="2">WARNING</td><td>'PULL UP'</td><td colspan="2">Repeated while in warning conditions</td></tr>
<tr><td>'TERRAIN'</td><td colspan="2">Repeated after leaving warning conditions</td></tr>
<tr><td colspan="4"></td></tr>
<tr><td colspan="4">MODE 3 - Altitude loss after takeoff</td></tr>
<tr><td colspan="4">Based on altitude loss after takeoff and go-around with flaps or landing gear not in the landing configuration</td></tr>
<tr><td>CAUTION</td><td colspan="3">'DON'T SINK, DON'T SINK'</td></tr>
<tr><td colspan="4"></td></tr>
<tr><td colspan="4">MODE 4 - Unsafe terrain clearance when not in landing config</td></tr>
<tr><td colspan="2">Landing Gear Up (Mode 4A)</td><td colspan="2">Landing Gear Down & Flaps not in landing position (Mode 4B)</td></tr>
<tr><td colspan="4">CAUTION</td></tr>
<tr><td>'TOO LOW TERRAIN'</td><td>'TOO LOW GEAR'</td><td>'TOO LOW TERRAIN'</td><td>'TOO LOW FLAPS'</td></tr>
<tr><td colspan="4"></td></tr>
<tr><td colspan="4">MODE 5 – Descent Below Glideslope</td></tr>
<tr><td>CAUTION</td><td colspan="3">'GLIDESLOPE'</td></tr>
</table>

Vertical Envelope

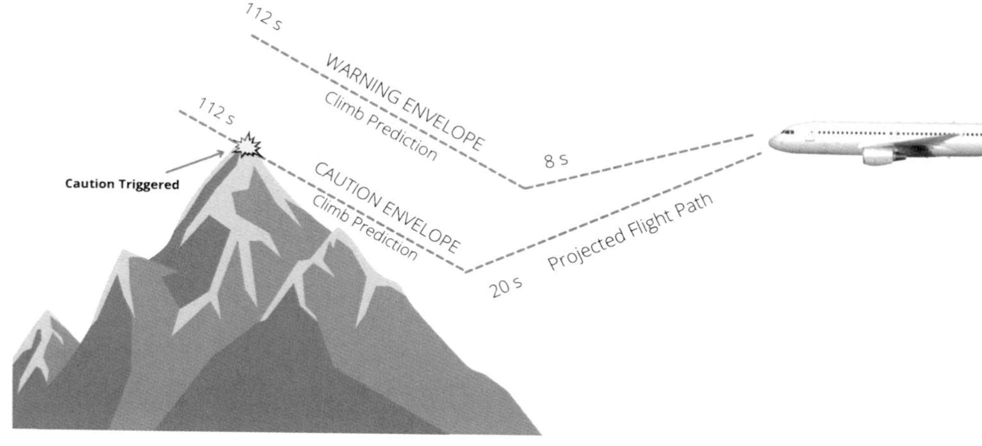

GPWS Overhead Panel

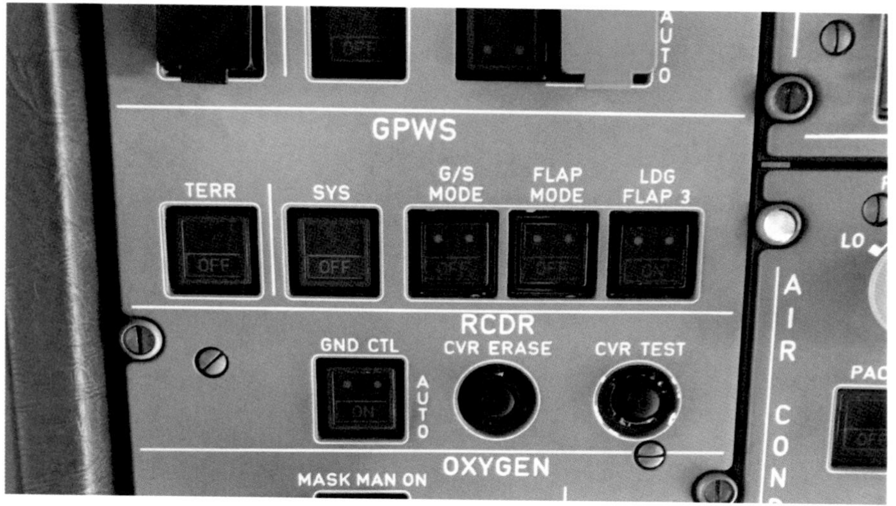

Failures

Unreliable Airspeed

The main reason for an unreliable airspeed indication is due to an obstruction of the pitot or static probes, this affects the readings in the cockpit which can be conflicting.

Systems on board use a logic data system whereby if one source of information differs from the other average values, then this source is not used.

At lower altitudes, most unreliable speed situations are permanent and due to obstructions such as foreign objects, severe icing or rain.

At high altitudes, most unreliable airspeed situations are temporary and are due to the same blockages, caused by temporary weather phenomena which will after time return to normal indications again.

Unreliable indications could be:

- Speed discrepancy
- Fluctuating airspeed / altitude
- Abnormal speed, altitude, pitch, thrust indications
- NAV ADR DISAGREE
- ANTI ICE ALL (CAPT + FO), (CAPT + STBY), (FO + STBY)
- Crew suspect incorrect data without ECAM
- STALL warning
- OVERSPEED warning

Priorities	
Fly the aircraft, silence any aural alerts.	
Memory items - IF NECESSARY	Close to terrain? Unsafe environment? Lost situational awareness?
Stabilise the aircraft	Memory items complete or if not, Level off to start troubleshooting
A/P, A/THR, FD	OFF - Prevents flight guidance system from using incorrect information.
Below FL250	Use the BUSS (Backup Speed Scale)
Above FL250	Use QRH Pitch / thrust table GPS Altitude can be used to confirm level flight. (Displayed on PFD when BUSS activated

Troubleshooting
Crosscheck speed and altitude with CAPT PFD, STBY, FO PFD *CAUTION - 2 or 3 ADR's can provide incorrect information, if unsure use the QRH Pitch / Thrust table or the BUSS*
Once identified, turn off the faulty ADR and complete the associated ECAM procedure
The QRH procedure includes the necessary steps to go through, once stabilised it is worth running through this to ensure you have the correct result.

If the faulty ADR still cannot be identified, use the ADR 1+2+3 FAULT procedure to set the aircraft up for landing.

Memory Items	
AP / FD	OFF
A/THR	OFF
Below THR RED ALT	15° / TOGA
Above THR RED ALT	10° / CLB
Below THR RED ALT	5° / CLB
FLAPS 0 - 3	Maintain
FLAPS FULL	Select CONF 3
SPEEDBRAKES	Retract
Landing Gear	Retract

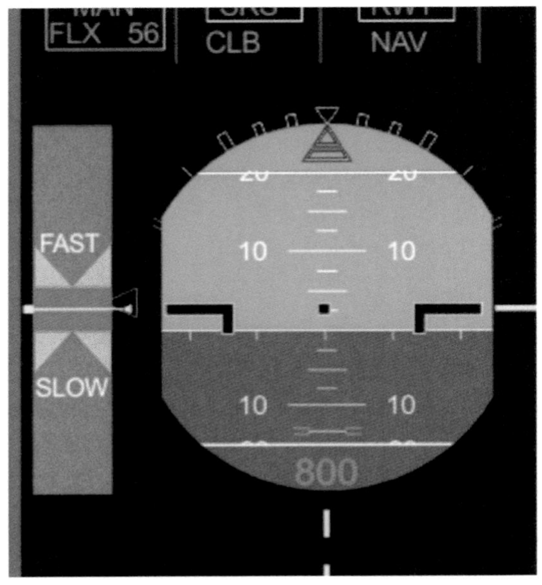

Backup Speed Scale (BUSS)

Dual Rad Alt Failure

The radio altimeters provide information to GPWS, FWC, AP, A/THR and flight control laws.

Threats
GPWS is fed from RA1, therefore GPWS is inop and terrain awareness becomes vital
CAT 1 only - 200 ft / 550 m
LOC mode only, ILS APP cannot be engaged
No auto call-outs so monitor 'FLARE' and closure rate at landing

Approach
Use Flap 3
GPWS Flap 3 pb - ON
APPR Speed - VREF + 10 kts
Landing Distance Procedure - Apply
LOC only approach and minima used
When gear down - Direct Law USE MAN PITCH TRIM - Displayed - trim the aircraft manually *This may trigger a configuration warning, be prepared and cancel using the EMER Cancel pb*

The final stage of the approach should be flown in raw data. This will reduce the risk of excessive roll is the LOC is engaged still.

OXYGEN

There are 3 different oxygen systems on the A320.

Cockpit Fixed Oxygen	Supplies oxygen in the event of de-pressurisation or smoke / fumes
Cabin Fixed Oxygen	Supplies oxygen for passengers and crew in the event of de-pressurisation
Portable Oxygen	Provided in the cockpit and also in the cabin to be used for emergencies and also for first aid

<u>Cockpit Oxygen</u>

Cockpit Oxygen is supplied via a high pressure cylinder which can be found in the lower fuselage. A pressure regulator allows the appropriate amount of oxygen to be used and this is controlled by 2 over-pressure safety systems which can vent the oxygen overboard if pressure becomes too great.

On the overhead panel is the CREW SUPPLY oxygen pb. When selected ON, this opens the valve and supplies low pressure oxygen to the masks.

There are generally 3 full face, quick donning masks in the cockpit. To use, the red grips need to be squeezed together whilst pulling the mask from the container, this action inflates the harness and will deflate to the appropriate pressure once on the head and grips released

The pressure regulator consists of 2 red grips as mentioned to inflate the mask and remove from the mask stowage compartment.

The emergency pressure selector is used to over-pressure the mask in case of fogging or to eliminate condensation and prevent smoke or smells from entering. If the red knob is pressed, it will over pressure for a few seconds only. If the knob is turned, a permanent over-pressure will be created.

Over-pressure is automatically enabled when cabin altitude exceeds 30,000 ft and when the N/100% selector is at the 100% position.

When down in the 100% position, the mask delivers 100% oxygen

When up in the N position provides a mixture of air and oxygen. This oxygen level increases as cabin altitude increases.

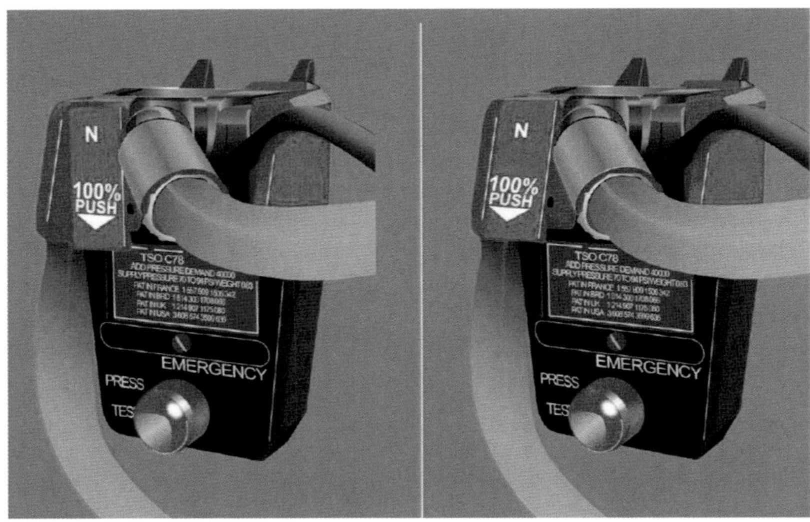

Oxygen Overhead Panel

Cabin Oxygen

Cabin oxygen is supplied via a fixed oxygen system using chemical generators. Each one of these generators can supply 2-4 masks. If the cabin altitude rises above 14,000ft, masks will automatically drop via an electrical latch. This can be over-ridden with the MASK MAN ON pb in the cockpit.

Masks can be found above passenger's seats, in the toilets, in each galley and at the station of each cabin crew.

Once the passenger pulls the mask, the supply of oxygen will start. There may be a smell of burning or an increase in heat due to the chemical reaction used to create the oxygen. These masks then supply pure oxygen for between 12-22 minutes, allowing the aircraft to descend to a safer altitude.

A manual release tool allows the cabin crew to open the doors manually if there is an electrical failure and the masks do not deploy.

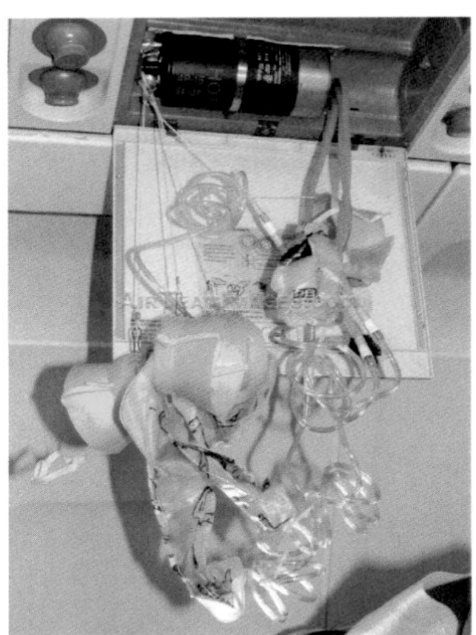

Portable Oxygen

Portable Oxygen can be found in the cockpit. This portable breathing equipment is a hood which can be used by a flight deck member when tackling a fire or smoke. This uses a chemical air regeneration system which allows the user to breath in regenerated air, and exhale to the regeneration system. This hood should allow for around 15 minutes of operation. Some smoke hoods contain an oxygen cylinder and also a CO_2 absorption system and this can be used also for around 15 minutes.

Cabin crew have use of portable oxygen bottles which provide 100% oxygen. These have a HI and LO flow rate which allows either 40 minutes or 70 minutes of oxygen. There are various types of bottles however most will have a tube/mask attached, a pressure gauge and an ON/OFF valve. These bottles should generally be more than ¾ full prior to departure.

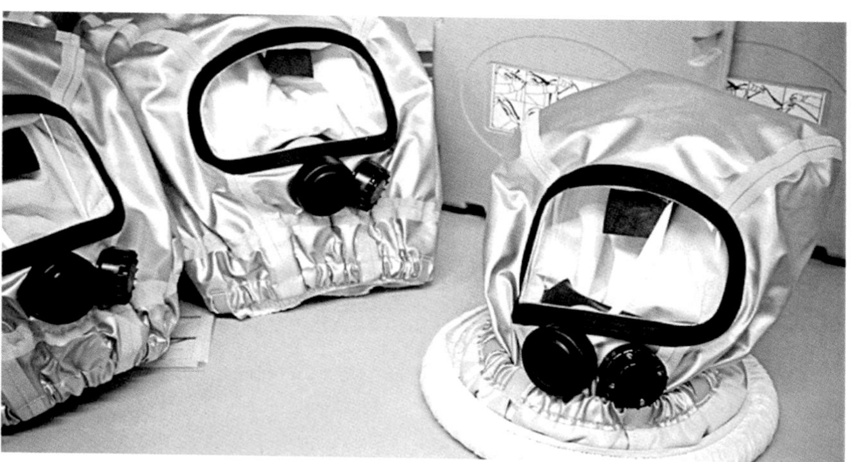

Protection after loss of Cabin Pressure – NORMAL Position	
During Emergency descent for all flight deck crew and observers	13 Minutes 15 Minutes (A320/A321NEO)
During Cruise at FL100 for 2 crew members	107 Minutes 105 Minutes (A320/A321NEO)
Protection against smoke with 100% oxygen for all flight deck crew and observers at 8000ft cabin altitude for 15 minutes.	

REF Temperature		°C	-10	0	10	20	30	40	50
		°F	14	32	50	68	86	104	122
MIN CAPT Indication (PSI)	CAPT		460	480	500	520	540	550	570
	CAPT + 3rd Occ.		650	680	700	730	750	780	800
MIN F/O Indication (PSI)	F/O		460	480	500	520	540	550	570
	F/O + 4th Occ.		650	680	700	730	750	780	800

Questions & Answers

Q. How long does the passenger oxygen last for?
A. Around 13 - 15 minutes

Q. Do the passenger oxygen masks generate oxygen immediately?
A. Oxygen is only generated when the mask is pulled towards the passenger

Q. Which ECAM page will display the oxygen pressure remaining?
A. The Door SD page

Q. How long does oxygen flow for in portable breathing equipment?
A. It lasts for approximately 15 minutes

Q. When do the passenger oxygen masks drop down?
A. When the cabin altitude reaches around 14,000 ft

Q. On crew oxygen masks, what does the emergency pressure selector do?
A. It provides an over-pressure in the mask which reduces fogging of the mask and eliminates any smoke or fumes also.

Q. What does the 'N' mean on the oxygen masks?
A. With the selector in the N position, the crew member will breathe a mixture of Oxygen and air. Above 35,000 ft cabin altitude, this will be pure oxygen.

Q. There is a yellow blinker next to the oxygen mask stowage, what does this indicate?
A. This indicates that oxygen is flowing to the mask.

Q. How does the crew oxygen and the passenger oxygen differ?
A. Passenger oxygen is provided via a chemical oxygen generator. Crew oxygen is provided using an oxygen cylinder.

PNEUMATIC

The pneumatic system provides high pressure air for the following:

- Air Conditioning
- Wing Anti Ice
- Water Pressurisation
- Hydraulic Reservoir Pressurisation
- Engine Starting

There are 3 sources for this high pressure air which is:

- Engine bleed systems
- The APU
- High Pressure Ground Air

A cross-bleed ducts connects the engine bleed systems as well as APU and ground HP air when available. A cross-bleed duct allows both sides to be interconnected or isolated.

2 Bleed Monitoring Computers (BMC) control the pneumatic system, if one fails, the other can take over. Each engine bleed system does the following:

- Select a compressor stage to use for bleed air
- Regulate the bleed air pressure
- Regulate the bleed air temperature

Normally, air is bled from the intermediate Pressure stage (IP) of the high pressure compressor. The HP valve will close if it detects low pressure upstream or excessive pressure upstream. The bleed valve acts as a shut-off and pressure regulating valve, maintaining pressure at 45 PSI.

The bleed valve is closed pneumatically if:

- Upstream pressure goes below 8psi
- There is return flow

The bleed valve is closed electrically if:

- BLEED pb is selected off
- ENG FIRE pb selected
- BMC detects:
    - Over-temperature
    - Over-pressure
    - Leak
    - Open Starter valve
    - APU bleed ON

A pre-cooler downstream regulates the temperature of bleed air. This uses cooled air from the engines fan to regulate temperature to around 200°c.

Air from the APU compressor is available on the ground and in the air to supply the pneumatic system. APU bleed air has priority over engine bleed air, whilst the APU bleed is selected ON, then engine bleeds will be closed.

Pneumatic / Bleed System SD Page

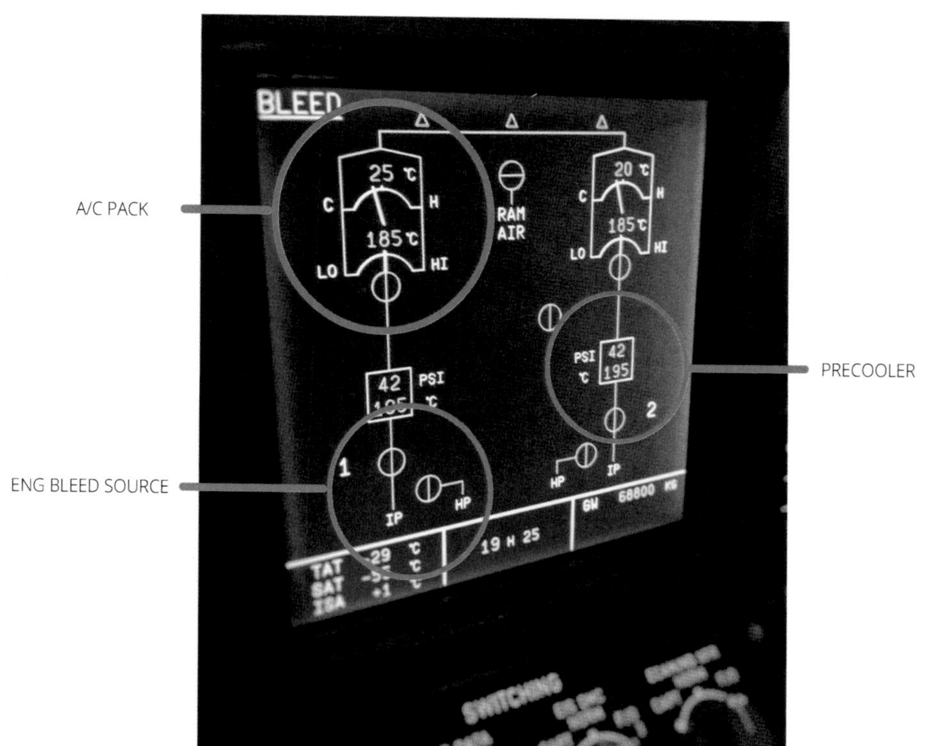

A320 / A321 NEO Pneumatic System

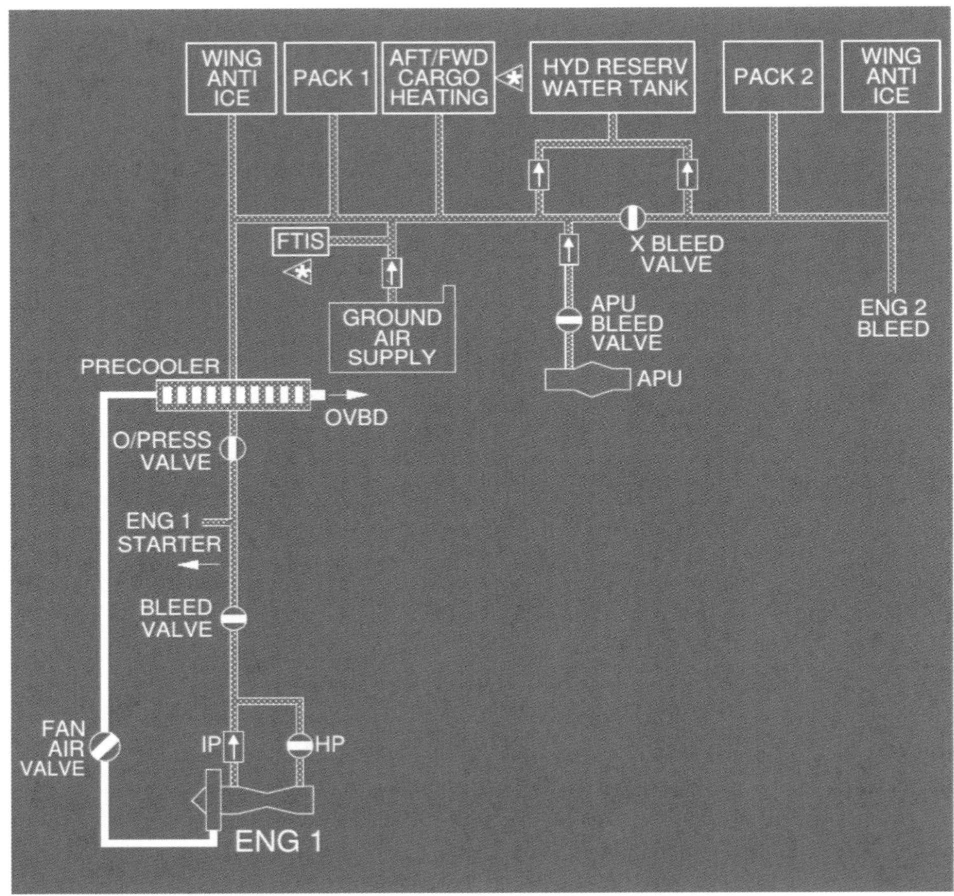

APU

The Auxiliary Power Unit is a small gas turbine jet engine in the rear of the aircraft which supplies electrical and pneumatic power.

On the ground it supplies electrical power for the aircraft and provides bleed air to start engines and to supply the air conditioning system.

Generally, the APU is turned off from engine start until after landing, however it can be used in flight as a back-up generator or to gain maximum aircraft performance.

The APU bleed system is fully automatic and the APU speed is always set to 100%. The bleed air cannot be used for wing anti ice due to no temperature regulation of the bleed air which could potentially damage the slats.

The APU can be started via the DC aircraft batteries. When the MASTER SW is pressed, electrical power goes to the APU which then performs a power up test. The air intake flap opens ready for the start sequence.

When the START button is pressed, the starter is energised then ignition turns on. Once above 95% the APU can supply bleed air and electrical power.

When shut down, the APU will run for a cooling period of 60 - 120 seconds if the bleed air was used.

The APU is capable of an auto shut-down procedure. This will trigger if any of the following occur:

- APU SHUTOFF sw on the external power panel pushed
- APU FIRE pb pushed
- An APU fire on the ground is detected

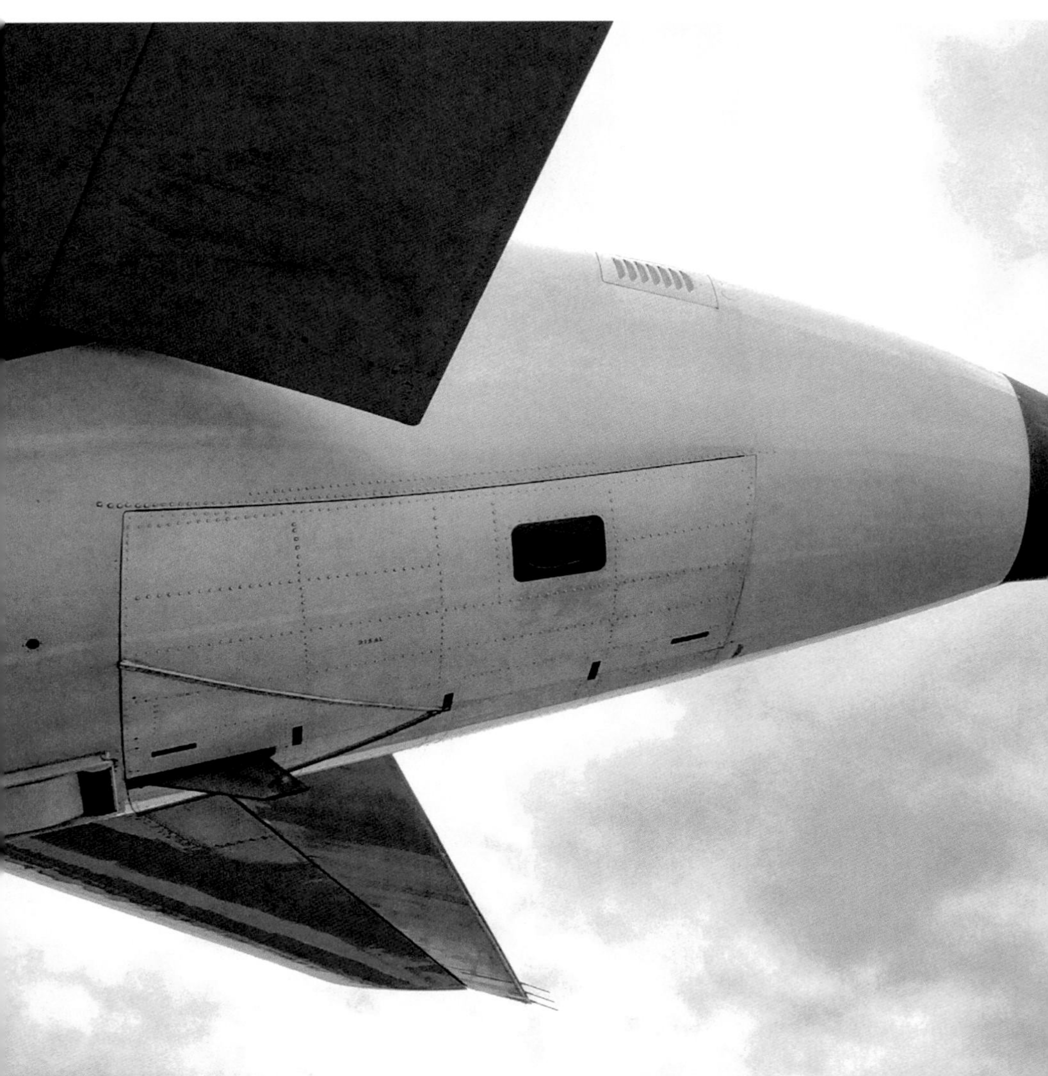

Limitations	
After 3 start attempts, crew must wait 60 minutes before another attempt.	
APU Bleed Use:	
Max altitude to assist engine start	20,000 ft
Max altitude for A/C & Pressurisation single pack	22,500 ft
Max altitude for A/C & Pressurisation dual packs	15,000 ft
Operational & re-start ceiling	39,000 ft
APU Elec Power	39,000 ft
Max N Rotor Speed	107 %

Questions & Answers

Q. Can APU be started and operated if LOW OIL LEVEL ECAM advisory is displayed?
A. If there is no Oil Leak, the remaining oil quantity allows normal APU operation for about 10 hours.

Q. Can you use the APU for Wing anti-ice?
A. No

Q. In the case of an APU FIRE, does the APU automatically shut down in the air or on the ground?
A. On the ground

Q. On battery power only, when you do an APU fire test, what are the indications?
• APU FIRE pb illuminated in red • SQUIB and DISCH light illuminated

Q. How many APU fire bottles are there?
A. One

Q. When does the START switch ON light extinguish?
A. The ON light on the START switch extinguishes 2 seconds after N reaches 95 % or when N is above 99.5 %

Q. What happens when you select the APU MASTER SW to OFF?
• The ON light on the MASTER SW P/b S/w, and the AVAIL light on the START P/b, go out. • The APU keeps running for a cooling period of 120 s at N 100 % speed • At 7 % the air inlet flap closes.

Q. How long will it take for the APU flap to fully close?
A. The air intake flap closes fully in approximately 20s.

POWERPLANT

All A320 engines are turbofan engines and all have the following:

- Engine with high bypass ratio
- FADEC - Full Authority Digital Engine Control
- Fuel system
- Oil system
- Air system
- Thrust Reverse system
- Ignition / Start system

CFM56 Engine

Engine

There are many types of engine available but most will have a Low pressure and a High pressure compressor turbine assembly.

Operation
The LP compressor will compress air which is then divided in two flows. Most air flows out of the core engine and provides most of the thrust. Remaining air will enter the core engine.
The HP compressor will compress that air entering the core engine.
Fuel is then mixed to this compressed air and is then ignited in the combustion chamber.
The resultant gas then drives the HP and LP turbines

N1 - Rotation speed of the fan - Used by FADEC to compute thrust

N2 - Rotation speed of the HP rotor.

At the bottom of each engine lies the Accessory Gearbox. This drives many accessories with mechanical power via the HP shaft. The gearbox of each engine operates:

- Pneumatic starter for engine start
- FADEC alternator for FADEC electrical power
- Engine driven generators
- Engine driven hydraulic pumps for Green and Yellow systems
- Engine fuel pump supplying combustion chamber with fuel
- Oil feed pump providing the oil system with oil

FADEC

FADEC is a system that offers full control of the engines and management of them. Each engine has a FADEC system mounted on the fan case.

Functions of FADEC
Control of gas generator - Fuel flow, Idle setting, turbine clearance, acceleration / deceleration schedules.
Protection from exceeding limits - N1, N2 overspeed, EGT during start.
Power Management - Thrust rating, manual thrust setting, A/THR demands
Automatic engine start - Ignition, start valve, HP valve, fuel flow, abort / recycle
Manual engine start - Start valve, HP valve, ignition
Thrust reverser - Actuation of doors, engine setting during reverse
Fuel re-circulation - re-circulating the fuel to the tanks

FADEC has 3 idle modes:

Modulated	Regulated due to bleed demand and ambient conditions
Approach	In flight with flaps extended, allows the engine to accelerate rapidly from idle to GA thrust
Reverse	Selected on the ground, a little higher than forward thrust

Fuel

Fuel is supplied to the combustion chamber at a pre-determined flow rate, pressure and temperature. Fuel generally travels from the tank, via a fuel pump and oil/fuel heat exchanger, then to a unit to control the fuel flow rate (Hydro-mechanical Unit) and finally to the fuel nozzles.

As the fuel is generally very cold, some is used to cool down the IDG's, this fuel then returns to the fuel tanks and helps to warm the remaining fuel in the tank.

At low thrust, if oil through the IDG is too hot, the cooled fuel is sent back to the tank at 300 kg/h. If the oil temperature rises, N2 is increased and fuel flow can reach 600kg/h depending on the fuel return temperature.

This re-circulation is inhibited at engine shutdown and during takeoff & climb when:

- Wing tank fuel is below 300 kg
- Fuel overflow in the surge tank
- Fuel feed by gravity only

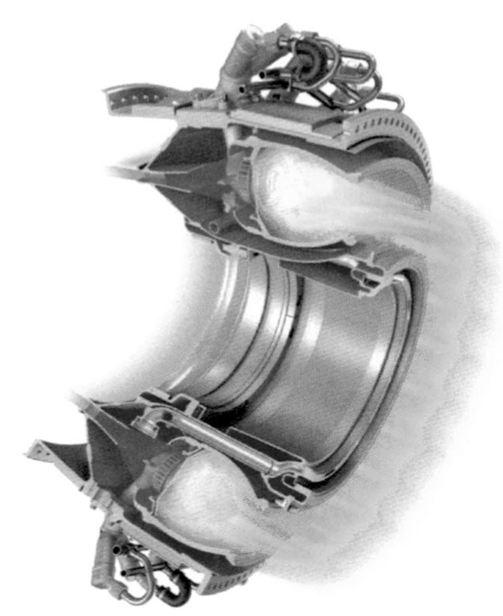

Oil

Oil is used to lubricate the engine components. The Oil system contains the following:

- Oil tank
- Lube / Scavenge pump modules
- Oil / fuel heat exchanger
- Filters, chip detectors, relief / bypass valves

A320 NEO / A321 NEO Oil System

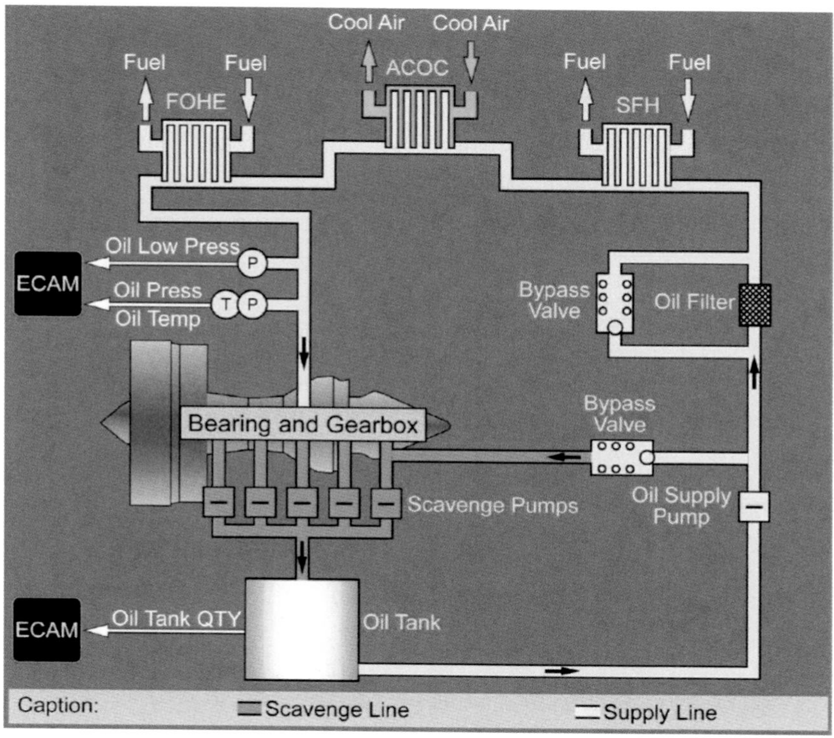

Air

The air bleed system supplies compressed air to the pneumatic system and also cools the engine compartment and the turbines.

Air is also used to assist cooling and control the clearance of the HP compressor and the stator case. A similar system is used to control the clearance of the HP turbine and LP turbine clearance by modulating the HP compressor bleed air flow and fan bleed air flow.

LEAP 1A Engine

Thrust Reverse

The reverse thrust concept is achieved by deflecting airflow forwards, thus enabling a greater stopping effect of the aircraft. Airflow is deflected via blocker doors controlled by a hydraulic actuator. These doors deflect the airflow via sleeves or bucket style doors.

Each thrust reverse system has the following:

- 4 Actuators
- 4 latches
- Door position switches
- Hydraulic control unit

The hydraulic control unit pressurises the thrust reverse hydraulic system, supplies the actuators with hydraulic power and also regulates the speed of the blocker doors. The total actuation time is less than 2 seconds.

In order for the reverse thrust system to deploy, the following logic occurs:

- One FADEC channel with associated throttle reverse signal
- Both main gears compressed - signal from LGCIU
- Thrust lever angle signal from at least one SEC

FADEC will limit the thrust to IDLE in case of accidental deployment of reverse thrust.

Ignition

The ignition system is controlled via the FADEC and each engine has 2 identical igniter systems A & B for each engine. The system controls the start valve, igniters and the HP fuel valve. Each FADEC controls a single igniter system in normal operation, however both systems can be controlled via a single FADC system in abnormal situations.

An automatic start uses a single igniter which is energised at around 16% N2 and de-energised at around 50% N2.

Start sequence:

- ENG MODE selector set to IGN - closes the pack valves
- Set ENG MASTER to ON
- LP fuel valve opens
- Engine start valve opens
- Ignition starts above 16% N2
- HP fuel valve opens
- Ignition stops above 50% N2
- Engine start valve closes and pack valve re-opens
- ENG MODE selector set to NORM

Dry cranking is used to ventilate the engine to remove any fuel vapour after an un-successful start attempt.

Thrust Lock
When auto-thrust is disconnected by the FCU button or a failure, thrust is locked at the current setting at time of disconnection

Alpha Speed / Lock
Inhibits flap retraction at a high angle of attack or low airspeed

Alpha Floor
Angle of attack threshold is reached and TOGA thrust is commanded

TOGA Lock
When TOGA is commanded, TOGA LOCK appears on the FMA. Recovered by selecting A/THR off using instinctive pb on thrust levers

FLEX TEMP
A de-rated thrust setting is used to prolong engine life, reduce noise and maintenance costs. It is calculated using air temperature, which produces less thrust as temperature increases. FLEX is the highest temperature that the engines would produce the required thrust for takeoff. This is affected by runway length, wind speed / direction and aircraft weight.

Minimum FLEX
Cannot be lower than the actual outside air temperature or the flat rating temperature: A319 - ISA + 30° A320 - ISA + 29° A321 - ISA + 15°

Limitations	
TOGA All Engines	5 minutes
TOGA Single Engine	10 minutes
MCT	No limit
Max Oil Temperature	140°c
Min Oil Temperature	-40°c
Start Attempts	3 attempts with a 20s pause
	15 minute cooling period between 4 failed starts
Reverse Thrust	Not to be used below 70 kts

Questions & Answers

Q. What happens when you hold the instinctive disconnect push buttons for more than fifteen seconds on THR LEVERS?
A. The A/THR system is disconnected for the remainder of the flight. All A/THR functions including ALPHA FLOOR are lost, and they can be recovered only at the next FMGC power-up on the ground.

Q. You are about to take off and have not inserted a FLEX temperature, can you still takeoff?
A. Yes, by selecting TOGA.

Q. Is there a mechanical connection between the thrust lever and the engine?
A. No

Q. How the thrust is controlled with the A/THR active?
A. In the auto thrust mode, the FMGC computes the thrust, which is limited to the value corresponding to the thrust lever position, unless the alpha-floor mode is activated.

Q. How the thrust is controlled with the A/THR not active?
A. Each engine is controlled by the position of the thrust lever. The pilot controls thrust by moving the thrust lever between the IDLE and TOGA positions. Each position of the thrust lever within these limits corresponds to an EPR.

Q. What is by Approach Idle?
A. It Is regulated according to aircraft altitude, regardless of bleed system demand. It Is selected in flight, when the flaps are extended with FLAPS lever not at zero position. It Allows the engine to accelerate rapidly from idle to go-around thrust.

Q. What is LVR CLB?
A. Flashes in white (3rd line on the FMA) if the thrust levers are not in CL position while the aircraft is above the thrust reduction altitude with both engines running.

Q. What is LVR MCT?
A. It flashes in white (3rd line on the FMA) if the thrust levers are not in MCT position after an engine failure, with speed above green dot.

Q. What is LVR ASYM?
A. When one thrust lever is in the CL detent and the other one is out of detent, the 'LVR ASYM' amber message will come up on the FMA until both levers are set in the CL detent - only with both engines operative.

Q. If a thrust lever is set between two detents, what is the rating limit?
A. When a thrust lever is set between two positions, the FADEC selects the rating limit corresponding to the highest mode.

Q. During an engine start sequence, the grey background on the N2 disappears at around 57%. What does this indicate?
A. This indicates that the start sequence has been completed.

Q. What is the meaning of the 'AUTO CRANK IN PROGRESS' message appearing on E/WD during an auto start?

A. After any start attempt that is not successful, a dry crank automatically occurs. This auto dry crank sequence will be initiated by the FADEC and this is what the E/WD message means.

Q. During engine start, if the amber FAULT light illuminates on the ENG MASTER panel, what could have happened?

A. The amber FAULT light comes on, and a caution appears on ECAM, if there is:

- An automatic start abort
- A start valve fault
- A disagreement between the HP fuel valve position and its commanded position.

Q. What does EGT mean?

A. EGT is short for Exhaust Gas Temperature. This is the temperature of the gases escaping at the exhaust of an engine, the temperature at the outlet from the turbine is measured by thermocouples.

Q. What does EPR mean?

A. EPR is short for Engine Pressure Ratio. The EPR instrument provides a readout of the ratio of the turbine discharge total pressure to the compressor inlet total pressure.

Failures

ENG 1/2 FAIL

Maintain the basics and fly the aircraft. Aviate, Navigate, Communicate.

Engine failures put the aircraft in CAT3 Single capability.

ENG MODE SEL - IGN	This is done in order to turn on the ignitors, protecting the working engine.
THR LEVER - IDLE	Ensure positive confirmation before moving, use all available means to do this
IF NO RELIGHT AFTER 30 s	The FADEC should relight the engine within 30 seconds if there is no damage, otherwise the Master Switch can be switched to OFF
IF DAMAGE - ENG FIRE PB - PUSH	Damage can be assumed if a loud bang, vibrations or stalling occur. This can be linked to a quick decrease in N1 / N2 / EGT and also the fuel flow.
AGENT 1(2) DISCHARGE AFTER 10 s	This time allows for the N1 to decrease which will reduce ventilation and increase the effectivity of the discharging agent

The engine is now considered as secure and the aircraft in a safe configuration.

IMBALANCE - MONITOR	Monitor the fuel tanks for any potential leaks. Start a timer to remind you to come back to this. Once confirmed that no leak exists, a cross-feed of fuel may be required to preserve the remaining engine
TCAS MODE SEL - TA	This prevents an RA occurring that would not be able to be complied with.
AVOID ICING CONDITIONS	Due to complications using the Anti icing system

The aircraft now has only 1 bleed source from the remaining engine so this has to be used efficiently. The cross-bleed selector will most likely be in the AUTO position which will close the cross-bleed valve. If wing anti ice is used, it will provide asymmetric icing which could affect the aerodynamics of the aircraft - not good!

If the FIRE PB has been pushed, its associated engine bleed valve and pack flow control valve will be closed off, thus wing anti-ice will not be available. The only way in which wing anti-ice can be used is if both FIRE PB's have not been pressed, one pack is off (of the failed engine) and the X-BLEED is OPEN.

In some situations, it may be beneficial to have some extra performance using the APU bleed air. This can help the air conditioning and pressurisation in the event of a go-around and gain maximum performance from the remaining engine.

If no FIRE PB's have been pressed, the APU bleed air can be used without condition.

- If FIRE PB 1 pressed, you cannot use APU bleed air
- If FIRE PB 2 pressed, you must close the X-BLEED before its use.

The reason for this is the way the bleed system is designed, as you can see below, if the FIRE PB 2 is pressed with the X-BLEED valve closed, there is no problem. If the FIRE PB 1 is pressed however with X-BLEED open, air will be contaminated from the damaged engine.

<u>Bleed display SD page</u>

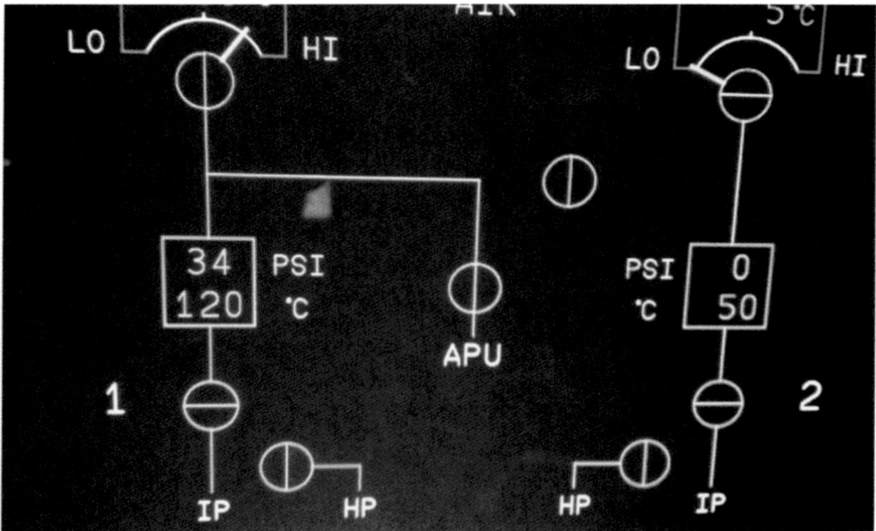

ENG Fail at takeoff:

Up to 100 kts, the takeoff can safely be aborted for any failure or abnormality.

Between 100 kts - V1, the takeoff should only be aborted for major failures including the following:

- Fire warning or severe damage
- Sudden loss of thrust
- Red ECAM warning
- Amber caution for engine or sidestick problems.

Initial Actions
Use rudder to maintain the centreline of the runway
Rotate to around 12.5°
Once airborne and safely climbing, GEAR UP
Maintain blue Beta target in the centre to ensure lateral stability
TOGA improves climb performance but is not a necessity

The pilot not flying will silence any aural warnings and will verbalise the failure, however no action will be taken until a minimum of 400 ft to ensure the aircraft is stabilised.

ENG Fail in the Cruise:

Immediate actions:

- Set both thrust levers to MCT
- Disconnect the ATHR and select speed - avoids thrust reduction
- Set a Heading and then Pull
- Check en-route MSA / PROG page and set an Altitude

Standard Strategy - (Terrain not an issue)
Speed - M0.78 / 300 kts - Within engine windmill re-light envelope
Do not decelerate below green dot speed
Set altitude as per the REC MAX EO cruise altitude from the PROG page
Maintain V/S 500 fpm and ATHR ON
Level off - set long range cruise performance located in the QRH
When time permits, complete ECAM procedure

Obstacle Strategy - (Maintain highest level if terrain an issue)
Set drift down ceiling located on PERF / CRZ page
Set Green dot speed - this reduces the rate and the angle of descent
When terrain threat is over, revert to standard strategy

Engine Tailpipe Fire

This will occur either at engine start or engine shut-down.

- Ensure MAN START pb is OFF
- Set ENG MASTER to OFF

Ideally the APU will already be running as this will be required to supply bleed air which will blow out the fire. If the APU is inop, the bleed source from the remaining engine can be used. Open the cross-bleed and set the remaining engine to 30psi.

- ENG MODE SEL - CRANK
- Select MAN START pb to ON

Once the fire has been extinguished:

- MAN START pb - OFF
- ENG MODE SEL - NORM

Do not press the engine fire pb's as this will cut power from the FADEC which is needed for dry cranking. Also, using the fire pb will render the engine unusable and major maintenance action will be needed.

Engine Vibration

An ECAM advisory will be shown when the vibration levels reach:

N1	➢ 6 Units
N2	➢ 4.3 Units

Vibrations alone may be a sign of potential engine problems but at the advisory stage, the engines only need to be monitored.

One cause of vibration can be icing on the fan blades, if icing conditions are likely to be the cause, follow the QRH procedure to shed ice.

If icing conditions are not present, monitor the vibrations. If they get worse,

consider reducing thrust but do not shut the engine down for this alone as you will loose all associated engine functions and redundancy.

Thrust Lever Malfunction

There are 2 Thrust Lever Angle (TLA) sensors per thrust lever (and per engine), these are linked directly to the FADEC. The two failures that can occur are:

ENG 1(2) THR LEVER DISAGREE	
On Ground	Affected engine IDLE power only
During Take off	TOGA / FLX maintained until thrust reduction
After thrust reduction in flight	Max available thrust is CLB
With slats retracted	Thrust limited to the larger TLA (limited to CLB)
A/THR - Keep on (Or select ON) A/THR manages thrust between IDLE and the higher TLA	
CONF 1 +	Affected engine IDLE power only (Even during a Go Around)

ENG 1(2) THR LVR FAULT	
On Ground	Affected engine IDLE power only
During Take off	TOGA / FLX frozen
After Slat retraction	MCT maintained in Manual thrust
A/THR - Select On If A/THR is engaged, it will maintain thrust between IDLE and MCT	
With CONF 1 +	Affected engine IDLE power only (Even during a Go Around)

With CONF 1+, the affected engine operates at IDLE power only and so the Approach, Landing and Go Around should be flown as Single Engine profiles.

WINTER OPERATIONS

The clean aircraft concept - this means that the aircraft should have no ice/ snow, slush or frost on its critical surfaces prior to takeoff.

It is the pilot's responsibility to visually check the following prior to departure:
Wings, Tail and control surfaces
Fuselage
Radome / Nose and flight-deck windows
Static ports & Pitot heads
Engine inlets, exhaust nozzles, cooling intakes, system ports/probes
Air conditioning inlets / outlets
Landing gear, gear doors & wheel bay
Fuel tank vents

The exception to the above is thin hoar frost up-to 3mm on the lower wing surface, fuselage, radome and engine cowl. Any markings or features must still be visible.

De-icing - Removing ice, snow, frost or slush from the aircraft surfaces by mechanical means or by a heated fluid.

Anti-icing - Applying a protective barrier to prevent ice or snow from forming on the surfaces. This is done using anti-ice fluid.

The following different liquids can be used:

- Heated water as part of a 2 step procedure
- Type 1 fluid
- Water and type 1 fluid mixture
- Type 2 or 3 fluid
- Water and type 2 or 3 mixture
- Forced air - Generally used for engine icing

Each liquid used will have a different lowest temperature to be used and also a Holdover time which must be checked to ensure the validity of the anti-ice procedure.

Type 1 fluid
Mixture of glycol and water and the colour orange. Applied hot and is used to de-icing.
Type 2 fluid
Colourless or a pale straw colour. Used as an anti-icing fluid and can be diluted with water.
Type 3 fluid
Emerald green in colour and used primarily as an anti-ice fluid.

Contaminated runway

A runway is considered contaminated when more than 25% of its surface is covered with a contaminant. These are generally classified as follows:

- Water
- Compacted snow
- Dry / Wet snow
- Slush
- Ice

We also classify the runway as either:

Damp	Not dry but water on surface does not cause a shiny appearance. Consider a wet runway for takeoff performance
Wet	Surface has a shiny appearance with a thin film of water not exceeding 3mm.

Each runway condition will have a particular crosswind limitation and performance data required for pre-take calculations. The main reason for calculating the contaminant type and depth is for calculating braking distance which is then used to calculate runway accelerate/stop distance, power thrust settings etc.

Takeoff Flap Setting

Low flap settings provide good climb performance, but with a longer takeoff distance - Best lift / drag ratio

High flap settings improve takeoff distance, however reduces climb performance.

Contaminated runways will most likely require a higher flap setting to reduce the stopping distance, but if any obstacles are nearby then this may have to be considered and potentially a lower flap setting used to improve the climb gradient.

Takeoff Speeds

A reduction of speeds is usually used to reduce the go-stop distances. On a contaminated runway, the screen height is reduced to 15ft rather than 35ft , this also allows for lower speeds to be used. Optimised speeds must be calculated based on local conditions and airports used. These speeds will always ensure a safety margin from:

- Stall speed
- Minimum unstick speed - VMU
- VMCA - Minimum control speed in the air
- VMCG - Minimum control speed on the ground.

FLEX takeoff is prohibited on contaminated runways.

Low Visibility Takeoff

Generally, the Captain will be pilot flying for a low visibility takeoff.

An RVR of 400 m or less is considered as low visibility. If no RVR information is available, the takeoff can only be carried out if the Captain is satisfied that the required RVR is available.

TOGA takeoff on contaminated runways required

Takeoff can be conducted to as low as 125 m if certain lighting is in force at the airport. These can include runway edge lights, centreline lights and possibly the requirement for an initial visual segment to be available. The first RVR may be replaced by pilot replacement.

Information can be found in the QRH and also the airport information pages specified ground equipment in use.

Threats
Ensure flight control checks are complete when stationary
If unsure on taxi routing, stop and confirm immediately
Once lined up, check heading and on correct centreline
At rotate, look inside the cockpit earlier as normal visual cues are not visible

Low Visibility Landing

When pre-flight, check that your destination and alternates have suitable performance criteria to ensure a safe landing. Obtain the runway condition as well as any contaminant in order to assess landing performance.

Care should be taken to assess the following:

- Wind speed and direction
- Braking action
- Runway length and width (cleared to full width?)
- Type and depth of contaminant

The Captain should always be the pilot flying if the runway is contaminated or a low visibility approach planned.

Consider all options for landing performance. If you are unhappy with anything, consider delaying the approach or diverting to a more suitable airport.

It is always advisable to carry extra fuel to deal with these options, however this extra fuel can cause the need for de-icing on the ground due to its extra weight and temperature.

An autoland cannot be carried out on a narrow runway

Autoland

Conducting an autoland requires planning and briefing of various points to ensure a safe outcome.

Preflight
If taking off in LVP's, ensure a takeoff alternate is selected within 320nm and 1 hours flight time with ideally, CAT 1 minima weather.
2 alternates must be selected when weather is below the minima of the destination instrument approach.

Aircraft technical status:

An A319/320 can autoland provided the FMA shows the following capability:

CAT2

CAT 3 SINGLE

CAT 3 DUAL

Check any defects that can affect the aircrafts landing capability.

Airport:

Check any NOTAMS relevant to RVR's not in use, runway closures, lighting downgrades or anything that could affect the airport capability.

Weather:

Check the actual and the forecast weather. Cloud base and RVR / visibility are the two pieces of vital information required to ensure the approach can be commenced.

Aircraft Setup
No DH entered in PERF page if CAT3 DUAL planned
DH value set if planning for CAT2 / CAT 3 Single
Check if red AUTOLAND light is functioning

Autoland 1000ft and below:	
1000 ft	All ECAM actions complete, configured, stable
900 ft	TCAS downgrades to TA only
800 ft	Landing inhibit until < 80 kts
700 ft	FMGC data lock - locks course, frequency, perf page
500 ft	Stable / Not Stable
350 ft	LAND - FCU modes locked, Check ILS course correct
200 ft	If AUTOLAND appears, go around
100 ft	Alert Height - Continue if Fail Operational
40 ft	FLARE displayed on FMA
30 ft	Thrust Idle
ROLLOUT	Check

Autoland Failures

<table>
<tr><td colspan="2">Above 1000 ft - Resolve any failures or go around</td></tr>
<tr><td>Between 1000 ft - Alert height - go around for any downgrade in capability which may include:</td><td>Alpha floor activation

AP disconnect - Cavalry charge

Loss of CAT3 - 3 clicks

Amber Caution - Single chime

Engine failure</td></tr>
<tr><td colspan="2">350 ft - If LAND does not appear, go around</td></tr>
<tr><td colspan="2">200 ft and below - go around for AUTOLIGHT light or:

Loss of autopilots

LOC deviation > 1/4 dot

G/S deviation > 1 dot

RAD ALT discrepancy > 15 ft

Long / early / untimely flare</td></tr>
<tr><td colspan="2">Flare height, go around if FLARE does not appear</td></tr>
</table>

As well as the failures above, if either pilot feels unhappy with the approach, then the safest thing to do is go around. Whilst pilots have to put trust in the aircraft capabilities and the ground equipment operating correctly, if the instinct of the pilot is questioned, then conduct a go around and then once in a safe environment, discuss the reason for the missed approach and plan the next option available.

FAILURE MANAGEMENT

Failure management is at the core of all simulator checks and line operations. However big or small an abnormal event may be, a structured approach is required to enable the problem to be solved effectively.

The main priority is to put the aircraft in a safe environment which will then enable you to deal with the issue.

Aviate, Navigate, Communicate... These are the initial actions involved with any failure and will ensure that you prioritise flying the aircraft and are in a safe environment to continue. Communicate with ATC and the cabin crew so that everyone is aware of the situation and also that you can keep interruptions to a minimum.

The following shows a breakdown of the basic structure that will allow failure management to be conducted in a safe way.

Master Warning / Caution - 'I have control'	
Aviate	AP/ATHR/FD, check speed, read FMA, attempt to re-engage AP, A/THR
Navigate	MSA, TCAS, Wx, ppos hold, continue SID, go-around
Communicate	'Attention crew at stations', Mayday/Pan, Sq 7700

A good idea also at this stage is to start a timer. This can be useful for establishing if a fuel leak has occurred as a result of a failure and useful if you need to balance fuel later in the flight. A timer can also give you a target to be down on the ground safely - 'We will aim to land within 30 minutes'.

Once the initial actions have been carried out and the aircraft is safe, the following process can be carried out:

Seatbelt Signs - ON
Announce failure - confirm using the SD page, overhead panel etc
OEB's - consider
'ECAM Actions' - Primary, Secondary failures
Status page - 'Stop ECAM', Consider checklist / resets / Advisories
Continue ECAM

Break down status into what affects you for cruise, approach, landing, go-around

- 'ECAM actions complete'

LAND ASAP - Aim to land within 30 Mins

LAND ASAP - Aim to land within 45 Mins

Time	Fuel or fire? Set stopwatch and use it to aim for a landing time / advise cabin crew of time available
Diagnose	'What do you think has happened?' Use SYS / Status pages. Ask cabin crew if they saw or felt anything? Check implications of the failure such as: Aircraft configuration for landing Aircraft landing category e.g. CAT1 only RWY length required Performance calculation Weather required
Options	Continue / Divert / Return Decide on the most suitable landing airport based on the above factors, as well as terrain or weather implications Consider short rwy + headwind VS long runway + crosswind
Decide	Least risk option, get going, direct to a hold or vectors for approach, 15nm file, MSA en-route, Plan B + C discussed
Assign	Depends on the failure and what is available FO to fly the aircraft and prep for approach Captain - Brief cabin crew / Passengers / Brief the approach and how it will be flown and managed
Review	Check if the original decision is still the safest Review Status page, overweight implications?

Approach	QRH gravity Gear / Flaps/Slats -5 kts, Alt-Direct law, VAPP, Long final, Land Assured, Start APU?
Landing	Heavy flight controls, visual aspect, nose high, fast, visual requirements, braking available, tug required, evacuation?
Go-Around	Flap/Slat configuration, speeds, fuel remaining, gear retract, another attempt?

ECAM WARNINGS / CAUTIONS

Any ECAM messages displayed to the pilots will be colour coded to allow the pilots to quickly identify the importance of the message.

RED	Requires immediate attention
AMBER	Awareness, no immediate action
GREEN	Normal operation
WHITE	Guidance for procedures
BLUE	Limitations or actions
MAGENTA	Specific messages

LEVEL 3	RED WARNING
Aircraft is in immediate danger and immediate pilot action is required to resolve	
Aural Warning	Continuous Repetitive Chime 'CRC'
Visual Warning	MASTER WARN Red light flashes System page automatically shows Warning message shown on E/WD

LEVEL 2	AMBER CAUTION
No immediate actions required however prompt management of the situation should be considered to minimize further failures	
Aural Warning	Single Chime 'SC'
Visual Warning	MASTER CAUT Amber light shows steady System page automatically shows Caution message shown on E/WD

LEVEL 3	AMBER CAUTION
Requires crew to monitor only	
Aural Warning	None
Visual Warning	Caution message shown on E/WD

Types of Failures

Primary	A failure on the aircraft or a piece of equipment affecting other systems or equipment
Secondary	Failure of equipment as a direct result of a primary failure
Independant	Failure of equipment or a system not affecting or degrading other systems or equipment

Continuous Repetitive Chime	
Associated with	Red Warnings
Duration	Permanent
Cancelled by	Pressing MASTER WARN

Single Chime	
Associated with	Anber Caution
Duration	0.5 s

Cavalry Charge	
Associated with	AP Disconnection via take over pb or failure
Duration	1.5 s / Permanent if due to failure
Cancelled by	Second push on takeover pb or MASTER WARN pb

Triple Click	
Associated with	Landing capability downgrade
Duration	0.5 s - 3 clicks

Buzzer	
Associated with	Cabin call - 3 s
EMER Cabin call	EMER CALL - 3 s, 3 times

MEMORY ITEMS

Loss of Braking

Reverse	MAX
Brake Pedals	Release - Pedal force when transferring to Alternate brakes is much more powerful
A/SKID & N/W STG	OFF - Reverts to Alternate
Brake pedals	Press - Apply with care
MAX BR PR Indicator	1000 psi - Monitor brake pressure
If still no braking	Parking brake - Short applications

Emergency Descent

Crew Oxygen Masks	ON
Signs	ON
Emergency Descent	Initiate ALT - Turn & Pull HDG - Turn & Pull SPD - Pull
FMA	Announce
If A/THR not active	THE LVRS - IDLE SPD BRK - FULL
When descent is established:	
Speed	Max *If structural damage suspected, set SPEED to prevent over-speeding and reduce stress on the airframe*
ENG MODE SEL	IGN
ATC	MAYDAY, state intentions
Transponder	7700 - Unless told otherwise
Crew Oxygen masks	Consider selector to N position to save oxygen
MAX FL / MEA	FL100 / MEA / MORA
If CAB ALT > 14,000 ft	PAX MASK MAN ON

When safe to do so, notify the cabin crew of the situation and when cabin oxygen is no longer required.

Stall Recovery

When the crew recognise a stall is about to occur via the aural warning or the stall buffet, apply the following:

PF - 'Stall, I have Control'	
Nose down pitch	Apply - Reduce angle of attack Thrust reduction may be necessary if no pitch control authority available
Bank	Wings Level
Minimising loss of altitude is secondary to reducing the angle of attack in order to regain lift from the wings.	
When out of the stall:	
Thrust	Increase smoothly
Speedbrakes	Check retracted
Flight path	Recover
If clean and below 20,000 ft – Flap 1 *This will increase the A of A margin of the stall*	

Stall Warning at Liftoff

This warning can be caused by a damaged angle of attack probe. If the crew experience this, immediately apply the following:

Thrust	TOGA
Pitch Up	15°
Bank	Wings level

Once a safe flightpath has been achieved and a safe climb is established, if the stall warnings continue then the pilots can assume a spurious warning has occurred. This could possibly be due to:

- Damage to one of the AOA probes
- Wake Vortex
- Ice formation around pitot
- Debris inside pitot tubes

Unreliable Speed

AP	OFF
A/THR	OFF
FD	OFF
Below thrust red alt	15° degrees / TOGA
Above thrust red alt / Below FL100	10° degrees / CLB
Above thrust red alt / Above FL100	5° degrees / CLB
Flaps 0 / 1 / 2 / 3	Maintain current config
Flaps full	Select config 3
L/G	Up

EGPWS

'PULL UP' - 'TERRAIN AHEAD PULL UP' - 'AVOID TERRAIN'	
Simultaneously apply the following:	
AP	OFF
Pitch	Full Up – pull to backstop and maintain
Thrust Levers	TOGA
Speedbrakes	Check Retracted
Bank	Wings Level

TCAS

Traffic Advisory Alert	
TCAS Mode	Check Armed - 'TCAS BLUE' 'TCAS I Have Control' Be prepared to take action
Resolution Advisory Alert	
TCAS Mode	Check TCAS mode follows RA orders
TCAS Mode not available	
AP	OFF
Both FD's	OFF
Vertical Speed	Adjust to fly within green area displayed on VSI
When clear of conflict:	
ATC	Notify
Flightpath	Adjust lateral and vertical guidance to resume normal flying in accordance with any ATC instructions
AP	ON
FD	ON

Windshear

'Windshear, TOGA'

Takeoff	Reject takeoff - alerts inhibited above 100 kts	
Airbourne	THR LVRS	TOGA
	AP	ON
	SRS	Follow
Landing	Go Around	Perform
	AP	Keep On

The aircraft will provide efficient aids to get out of the windshear situation, these include the use of:

- Alpha Floor Protection
- SRS AP/FD pitch
- High Angle of Attack Protection

Autopilot will disconnect if A of A goes above alpha prot

If no FD bars, pitch to 17.5°

International Standard Atmosphere - Due to the natural gaseous surroundings around the earth, an average condition is required to set a standard baseline to use. ISA is referenced at a sea level temperature of 15 degrees C and a pressure of 1013 hPa or 29.92 Hg.

Temperature decreases at approximately 2 degrees C per 1000 ft up to the tropopause. From the tropopause upwards, the temperature remains at around -56° degrees C.

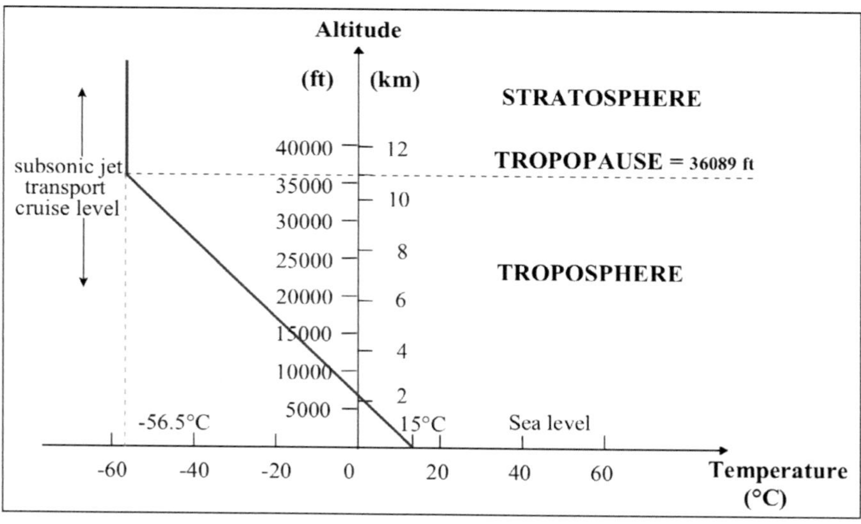

The indicated altitude is the vertical difference between the pressure surface where the ambient pressure is measured (aircraft location) and the reference pressure surface which is selected by the pilot.

QFE	Pressure at the airport reference point - Altitude above the airport.
QNH	Mean sea level pressure. Calculated using the pressure at the airport vs the mean sea level. QNH shows altitude above mean sea level.

Flight Level - Indicated altitude in feet divided by 100

Transition Altitude - Indicated altitude above which the standard setting must be used.

Transition Level - First available flight level above the transition altitude

If temperature is high - You will fly higher

If temperature is low - You will fly lower

Calibrated Airspeed - CAS

Obtained from the difference between the total pressure and the static pressure. This difference is called the dynamic pressure.

To measure total pressure - airflow is stopped using a pitot tube which will measure the impact pressure. This measurement will account for ambient pressure (static) at the given flight altitude plus the aircraft motion (dynamic)

Static pressure is measured using static probes which show the ambient pressure at the given aircraft altitude.

Indicated Airspeed - IAS

The actual speed of the aircraft indicated on the airspeed indicator - affected by angle of attack, flap configuration, wind direction or measurement errors. This is known as instrument correction.

True Airspeed - TAS

Represents the aircraft speed in an air mass which is itself moving compared to the earth below. Obtained by using the CAS, the air density, and a compressibility correction.

Groundspeed - GS

The aircraft speed in a fixed position - equal to TAS corrected for the wind correction.

Mach Number

Mach number is a comparison between the TAS and the speed of sound. Speed of sound is dependent on temperature. When the pressure altitude increases, the SAT decreases and thus so does the TAS.

Higher = Slower

Speeds

V1	Highest decision speed at which the crew can decide whether to reject the takeoff.
VR	Rotate speed - Aims to reach V2 at 35 ft latest after an engine failure
V2	Takeoff safety speed above 35 ft with one engine failed. Shown on speed scale by Speed Select symbol
VREF	Reference speed for final approach
VAPP	Final Approach Speed, calculated by FMGC. Equates to VLS + Wind Correction Wind correction minimum of 5 kts, maximum of 15 kts VAPP must not be lower than VLS + 5 kts
VA	Max design maneuvering speed - structural speed for full control deflection
VMCG	Minimum speed on the ground during takeoff at which the primary flight controls can control the aircraft in the event of engine failure.
VMCA	Minimum control speed in flight with one engine failed, the other at takeoff thrust and max bank of 5° - takeoff flap, gear retracted.
VMCL	Minimum control speed in flight with one engine failed, the other at takeoff thrust and max bank of 5° - takeoff thrust, approach flap.
VFE	Max speed for each flap configuration
VLE	Max speed with landing gear extended
VLO	Max speed for landing gear operation
VMO	Maximum Speed

Weights

Manufacturers Empty Weight - MEW

Weight of the structure, engines, systems and equipment integral to the aircraft. Includes fluids contained in closed systems e.g. hydraulic fluid.

Operational Empty Weight - OEW

Manufacturers empty weight plus the operator's items e.g. cabin crew, flight crew, emergency equipment, unusable fuel, engine oil, toilet chemicals, catering equipment, seats, documents.

Dry Operating Weight - DOW

Total weight of the aircraft excluding usable fuel and the traffic load. Includes flight specific items such as newspapers, catering etc.

Zero Fuel Weight - ZFW

The addition of the total traffic load (passengers, baggage, cargo etc) to the dry operating weight.

Landing Weight - LW

The weight of the aircraft on landing. Equal to ZFW plus fuel remaining.

Takeoff Weight - TOW

Equal to landing weight plus trip fuel or equal to ZFW plus takeoff fuel

TOW = DOW + traffic load +fuel reserves + trip fuel

LW = DOW + traffic load + fuel reserves

ZFW = DOW + traffic load

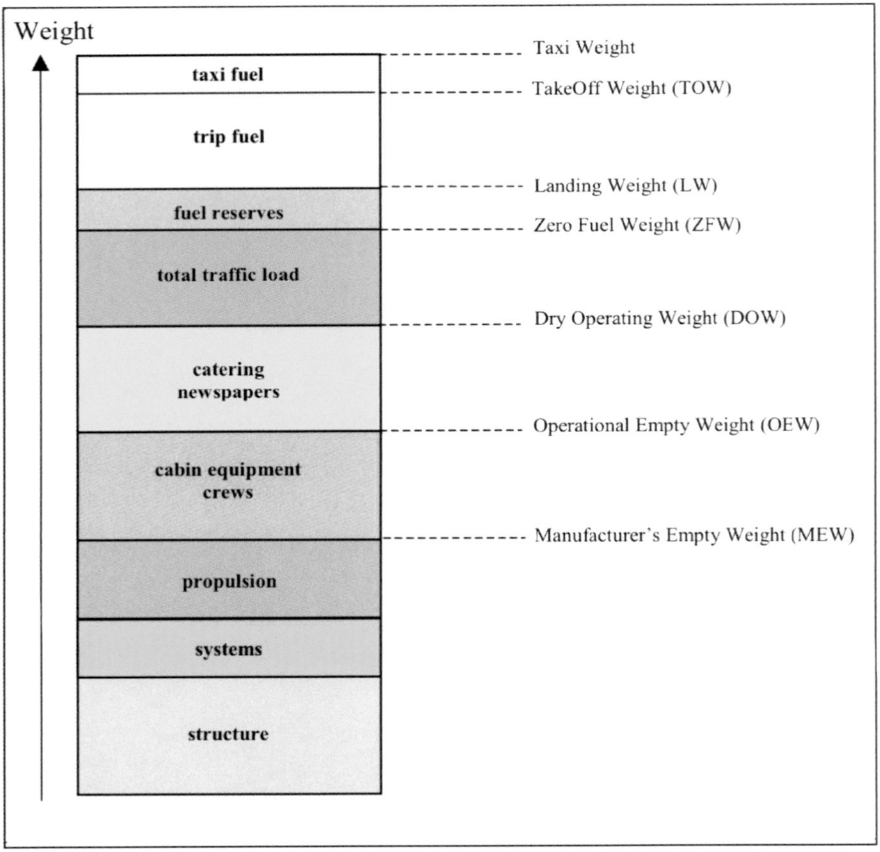

Weight

taxi fuel

trip fuel

fuel reserves

total traffic load

catering
newspapers

cabin equipment
crews

propulsion

systems

structure

Taxi Weight

TakeOff Weight (TOW)

Landing Weight (LW)

Zero Fuel Weight (ZFW)

Dry Operating Weight (DOW)

Operational Empty Weight (OEW)

Manufacturer's Empty Weight (MEW)

Decision Speed - V1

Maximum speed at which the crew can reject the takeoff and stop the aircraft within the safe limits of the runway length.

Rotation Speed - VR

The speed when the pilot initiates the rotation at around 3 degrees / second.

Takeoff Climb Speed - V2

The minimum climb speed that must be reached at a height of 35ft above the surface of the runway, incase on an engine failure.

Takeoff Run Available - TORA

Length of runway available suitable for the ground run on takeoff. Equal to runway length or the distance from the runway entry point if using an intersection.

Takeoff Distance Available - TODA

The extension of the runway by using the clearway area beyond the runway plus the TORA.

Accelerate-Stop Distance Available - ASDA

Extending the runway using the stopway which is the area beyond the runway. Calculated as the length of the takeoff run available plus the length of the stopway.

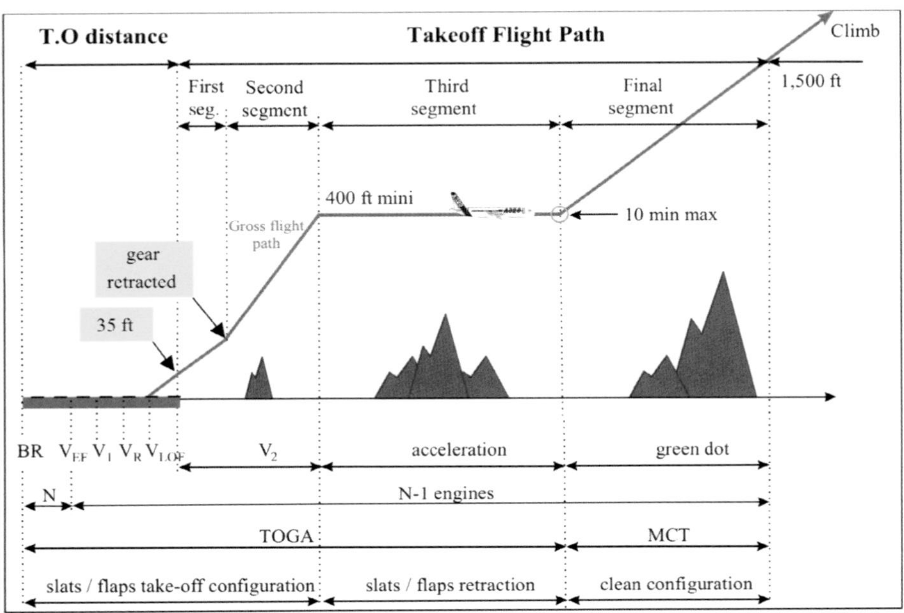

When pressure altitude increases:	Takeoff distance increases Climb gradient decreases MTOW decreases
When temperature increases:	Takeoff distance increases Climb gradient decreases MTOW decreases
Upward runway slope	Takeoff distance increases ASDA decreases
Downward runway slope	Takeoff distance decreases ASDA increases

Dry Runway	Neither wet or contaminated
Damp Runway	Surface not dry but moisture gives a shiny appearance
Wet Runway	Surface covered with water less than or equal to 3 mm, moisture on runway appears reflective without standing water
Contaminated Runway	More than 25% of the runway is covered by standing water, slush, Wet snow, Dry snow, compacted snow or ice

Flex Takeoff

The aircrafts actual takeoff weight is usually less than the max regulatory takeoff weight, this allows takeoff at a lower thrust than maximum thrust which increases engine life and reliability and reduces maintenance costs.

A reduced takeoff thrust is called a flexible takeoff and the thrust is called flexible thrust.

It is possible to determine the temperature at which the thrust needed for takeoff would be the maximum takeoff thrust for this temperature. This temperature is called flexible temperature.

		FIRST SEGMENT	SECOND SEGMENT	THIRD SEGMENT	FINAL SEGMENT
Minimum climb gradient (N-1) engines	Twin	0.0%	2.4%	-	1.2%
	Quad	0.5%	3.0%	-	1.7%
Start when		V_{LOF} reached	Gear fully retracted	Acceleration height reached (min 400 feet)	En route configuration Achieved
Slats / Flaps Configuration		Takeoff	Takeoff	Slats / Flaps retraction	Clean
Engine rating		TOGA/FLEX	TOGA/FLEX	TOGA/FLEX	MCT
Speed reference		V_{LOF}	V_2	Acceleration from V_2 to Green Dot	Green Dot
Landing gear		Retraction	Retracted	Retracted	Retracted
Weight reference		Weight at the start of the gear retraction	Weight when the gear is fully retracted	Weight at the start of the acceleration segment	Weight at the end of the acceleration segment
Ground effect		Without	Without	Without	Without

Takeoff Distance Available

Accelerate Stop Distance Available

Takeoff Run Available

Landing Distance Available

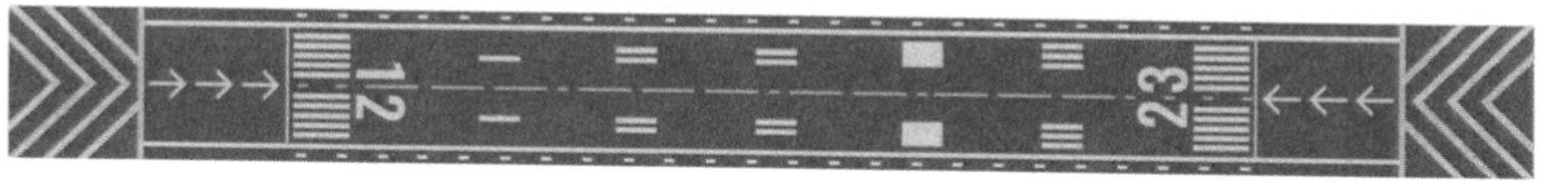

Clearway

Stopway

Landing Distance Available

<table>
<tr><td colspan="2">With no obstacles under landing path:

Landing distance available is the runway length - TORA</td></tr>
<tr><td colspan="2">With obstacles under landing path:

The LDA may be shortened</td></tr>
<tr><td colspan="2">Lowest Selectable Speed - VLS

Pilots should not select a speed below this.</td></tr>
<tr><td colspan="2">Final Approach Speed - VAPP

Landing speed 50 ft above the landing surface.</td></tr>
<tr><td colspan="2">VAPP = VLS + Wind Correction</td></tr>
<tr><td colspan="2">A minimum wind correction of 5 kts is normally applied with a maximum value of 15 kts</td></tr>
<tr><td>Upward runway slope</td><td>Landing distance decreases</td></tr>
<tr><td>Downward runway slope</td><td>Landing distance increases</td></tr>
</table>

Required Landing Distance

The reference used for dispatch landing performance, factored based on the following:

- Max manual braking after main gear touch down
- Max reverse thrust, maintained to 70 kts
- Antiskid and all spoiler's operative
- Regulatory dispatch factor

Dry Runway -

Aircraft landing weight must permit landing within 60% of the landing distance available at the destination and the alternate.

Wet Runway -

The required landing distance must be at least 115% of that of a dry surface.

Contaminated Runway -

The required landing distance must be at least or the greater of the required landing distance on a wet runway and 115% of the landing distance determined in accordance with approved contaminated landing distance data.

CEO / NEO DIFFERENCES

Cockpit Preparation

To view the Eng Oil Qty, the FADEC needs to be powered which is achieved using the FADEC pb's on the rear of the overhead panel.

Starting Engines

If previously flown, the LEAP 1A engine may require dry cranking to ensure the thermal state of the engine is correct prior to starting. This limits the engine core speed and limits N2 to 30%.

Minimum Oil Temperature for starting is -40°

Takeoff

At high temperatures, idle thrust may increase

Minimum Oil Temperature for takeoff is +19°

Landing

Ensure a cool down period of 3 minutes after landing for thermal stabilization.

Use of full reverse is much more effective than CEO models.

Additional

- FADEC automatically controls engine core anti icing
- RAD ALT auto callouts 2500 ft / 1000 ft
- Cabin Ready memo for cabin secure
- Runway Overrun Protection
- AP/FD TCAS equipped
- Turbulence Penetration Speed - 260 kts below FL200
280 kts above FL200

AUTO FLAP RETRACTION

When flying a departure at heavy weights and with speed constrictions it may be useful to use the automatic retraction system.

This is activated whilst in config 1 + F and at a speed of 210 kts (320) or 215 kts / 225 kts (321).

The system will automatically retract the flaps to 0° whilst keeping slats extended. This will change the VFE to the new restricted speed. When ready to accelerate, increase speed above S speed and then select Flap 0.

It may be wise to use selected speed here and to select a sensible speed below VFE until the slats have retracted fully, and then increase speed. This will ensure that an overspeed does not occur whilst the slats are transitioning.

The overspeed warning is based on the actual position of the Slats / Flaps and as such, the PFD may not show the speed in the red and black speed strip. All overspeed situations should be reported however in this case, it is not operationally significant.

As well as the above procedure, the A320 can also use the Alpha Lock function which will prevent slat retraction at a high angle of attack or a low speed situation. A. LOCK will pulse on the E/WD display and this will end and retract the slats when the angle and also the speed are back in normal limits.

TROPOPAUSE & ATMOSPHERE

The air above us can be categorized into different layers as summarized below:

Atmosphere

This air surrounds the planet closer to the surface and extends up to around 100 miles. This air mass is divided into two layers called the troposphere and the stratosphere. The area where they meet is known as the Tropopause and is generally considered to be at an average height of 36,000 ft, however this height does change (20,000 ft above the poles, 60,000 ft above the equator).

The 2 air masses can be the cause of jet streams and associated turbulence which needs to be considered for flight planning. Most weather is contained below the tropopause, however some convective weather patterns can go well above this layer and these should be avoided.

The FMGC will use data entered to predict wind values based on the wind and temperature entered in the INIT page. It will use the temperature based at an altitude associated with the tropopause to give an accurate temperature profile for planning.

The tropopause is also important to know incase of the fuel temperature decreasing and a need to descend into warmer air. Below the tropopause, a 4000 ft descent gives an increase in the TAT of around 6-7°c.

Troposphere

The Troposphere extends from the ground level to between 25,000 - 60,000 ft. Within this level, generally the temperature will drop at around 2°c per 1000 ft, this is called the lapse rate.

The tropopause varies with season, latitude and weather conditions. Typically, the temperature of the tropopause over the poles is around -50°c and over the equator, around -80°c. The troposphere is controlled by the amount of solar energy, thus is lower where the air is colder.

The tropopause is a region of turbulence due to the variations in vertical motions which occur above, at and below it. This is generally known as Clear Air Turbulence.

Another feature of the tropopause is that it acts as a barrier and helps prevent thunderstorms from rising above it. Only severe thunderstorms will have enough kinetic energy to penetrate it, before cooling takes place and it slows down.

Stratosphere

Above the Tropopause is the Stratosphere. Air in this layer remains at a constant temperature and does not decrease any further with height.

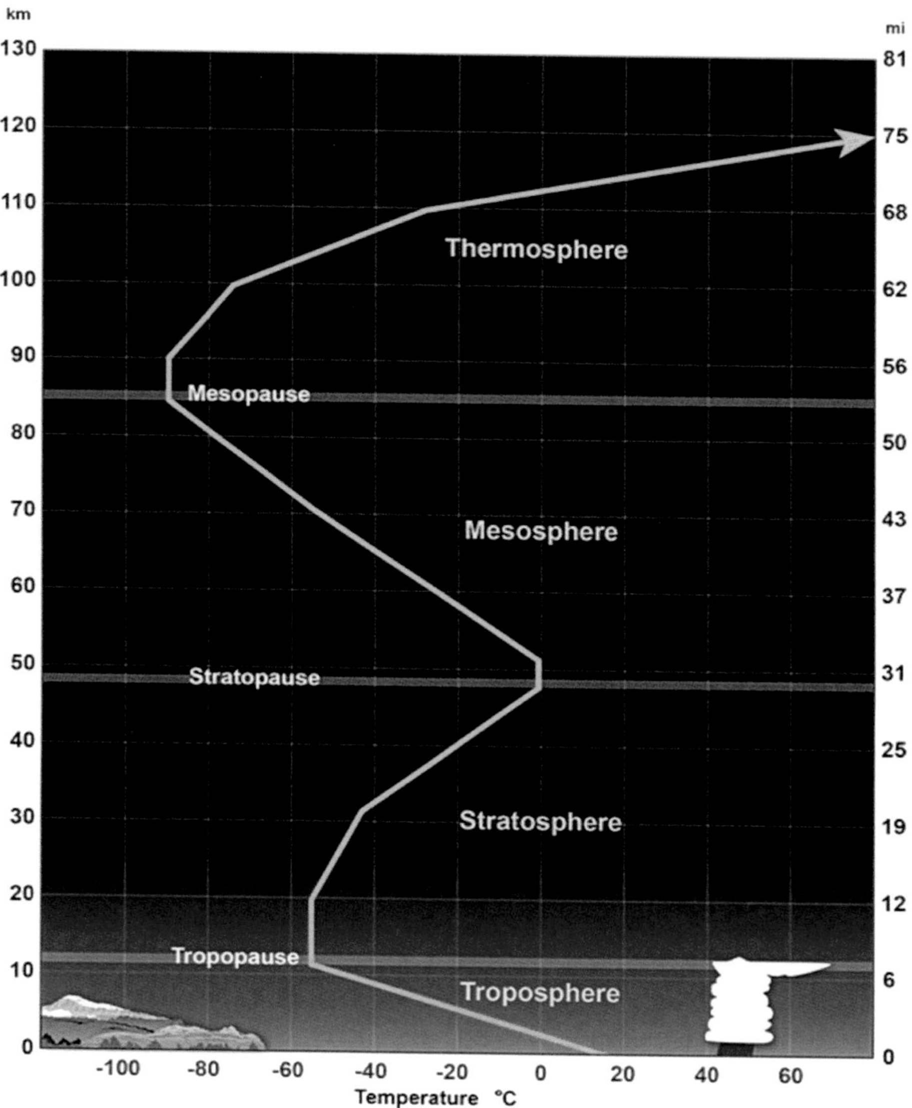
km
130
120
110
100
90
80
70
60
50
40
30
20
10
0
mi
81
75
68
62
56
50
43
37
31
25
19
12
6
0
Thermosphere
Mesopause
Mesosphere
Stratopause
Stratosphere
Tropopause
Troposphere
-100
-80
-60
-40
-20
0
20
40
60
Temperature °C

PERFORMANCE / IDLE FACTOR

Performance Factor

When aircraft are brand new, the engines have calculated values of their fuel burn based on a 'base model' which would be 0.0.

As the aircraft get older, the fuel consumption will very gradually degrade leading to an increase in fuel burn. This is measured as a 'monitored fuel factor' and this shows the actual fuel consumption of the engine compared to the base model.

The aircraft will then use this PERF Factor to predict the correct fuel flow for fuel predictions and computations to ensure they match with the actual fuel burn. A factor of +2.0 indicates that the aircraft fuel deviation is 2% compared to the 'base model'.

Idle Factor

The IDLE Factor is used to help compute the vertical profile in the descent phase from the Top of Descent to the first altitude constraint, based on a given thrust and speed.

IDLE Factor adds additional thrust to a given amount of thrust to maintain the vertical profile incase of windy conditions based on winds entered or uploaded.

If the IDLE Factor is positive, the profile is less steep and descent starts earlier.

If the IDLE Factor is negative, descent is steeper, descent starts later.

In DES mode, the aircraft will maintain the vertical profile and will use speed to regain the profile if needed.

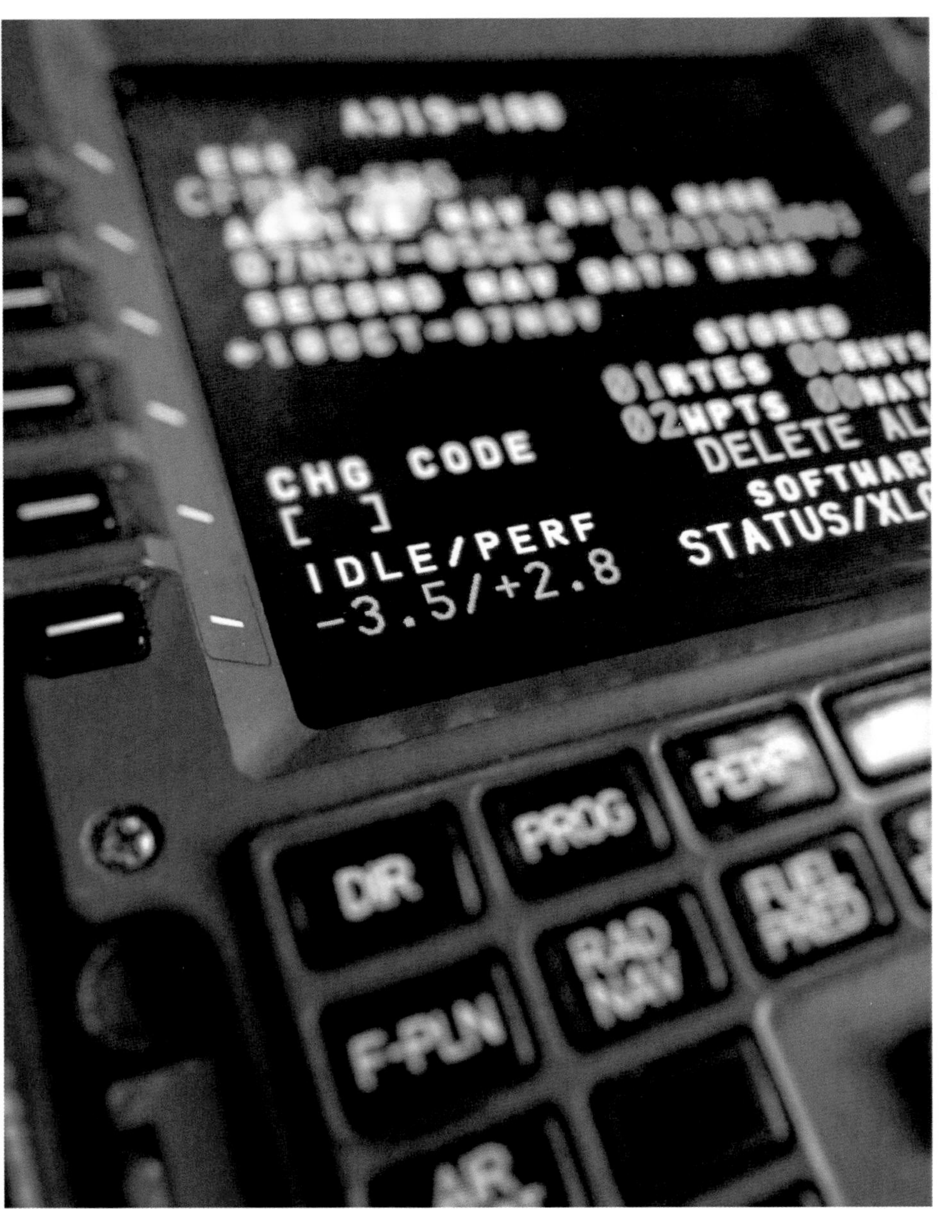
A319-100
SECOND NAV DATA BASE
STORED
RTES
WPTS
CHG CODE
[ ]
IDLE/PERF
-3.5/+2.8
PROG
DIR
RAD NAV
F-PLN

NAVIGATION ACCURACY

When briefing from the FMGC, it is often said that we have 'GPS PRIMARY' and NAV accuracy is HIGH - but what does this actually mean for us as pilots?

To calculate the aircraft position, each of the FMGC's uses a mixture of IRS position, Radio position or a GPS position. The FMGS will then select the most accurate position which is based on the accuracy of the equipment used. The order of priority of equipment is as follows:

- IRS-GPS
- IRS-DME/DME
- IRS-VOR/DME
- IRS Only

IRS Position

Three IRS's are used to compute a triangulated position known as the 'MIX IRS'. Each IRS can then select a GPS source to ensure the best availability and accuracy of this position.

Radio Position

Available nav-aids to use for radio position are:

- DME/DME
- VOR/DME
- LOC
- DME/DME-LOC
- VOR/DME-LOC

2 DME's can be used to calculate distance - if you imagine a circle around each DME station - where these circles meet, this gives a distance to use for calculations.

A VOR/DME can give a bearing and also a distance to use to help compute position.

Accuracy High / Low

The FMGS will check the position for inaccuracies and deviations and is generally an estimate of deviation used until the IRS's are next aligned. This is called the Estimated Position Uncertainty (EPU).

The required Navigation performance for the flight is compared with the estimated accuracy of the aircraft.

NAV ACCURACY HIGH	EPU does not exceed the RNP The FM position is accurate for the En Route criteria
NAV ACCURACY LOW	EPU exceeds the RNP Must compare raw data from tuned nav aids against FM data

GPS PRIMARY

GPS PRIMARY will be displayed on the PROG page when:

- The ability to detect a failure of the navigation position data - called integrity criterion.
- The NAV ACCURACY is shown as HIGH

If GPS PRIMARY is displayed, the crew are not required to carry out any navigation accuracy checks. If any of the following happen then navigation accuracy must be monitored:

- NAV ACCUR DOWNGRAD
- IRS Only navigation
- GPS PRIMARY lost on one ND
- PROG page displays LOW accuracy

Maximum Difference between Altimeters

CAPT PFD / FO PFD	+ / - 20 ft
PFD and Elevation	+ / - 75 ft
PFD and ISIS	+ / - 100 ft

EFFICIENT FLYING

As pilots and Airlines, we are becoming a lot more aware of our Carbon Footprint and using cost saving initiatives to reduce the impact aviation has on the environment. As fuel is one of most airlines biggest expenditure then using measure to reduce fuel usage should be looked at carefully.

Cost Index

Cost Index (CI) is used to define the relationship between time and cost when flying. It calculates the lowest cost per nautical ground mile enabling an optimum speed to be flown based on the weight and wind conditions. The FMGC calculates this and computes a resultant speed.

CI = kg / min or 100 lb / h

An increase in headwind will produce a speed increase.

An increase in tailwind will produce a speed decrease.

Also, when the aircraft flies at lower altitudes, the speed decreases to compensate for the increase in true air speed.

Cost Index - 0	Min fuel consumption, max range
Cost Index - 999	Minimum time

95% Stat Fuel

Statistical Contingency Fuel is added to some Airlines flightplans. This shows that 95% of all flights on that particular sector would likely land with alternate and final reserve fuel still remaining. This can be a key factor when deciding how much fuel to carry for the flight.

The fuel cost for carrying extra fuel can be calculated at around 4% of the weight, multiplied by the hours for which it will be carried.

E.g. Carrying an extra 400 kg for a 2 hr flight would cost around 32 kg in extra fuel to carry it.

APU

Delaying APU start whilst on the ground will save a lot of fuel. The APU will burn around 35% more fuel when the APU BLEED pb is turned ON - delay this until required for cabin comfort or engine start.

After the engines are shut down, the APU BLEED should be turned off, unless there is extreme weather or if the passengers are delayed disembarking the aircraft.

Single Engine Taxi

Starting only one engine and taxying towards the runway does save time, however judgement should be made for smaller airports so that pilots are not rushed or overloaded whilst taxying.

On average on a short haul sector, the average fuel saving for single engine taxi is around 18 kg.

To allow for thermal stabilization of the engine prior to takeoff, the second engine must be started at least 3 minutes prior to takeoff. On landing, a time of 3 minutes must have passed to allow the engine to cool down before single engine taxi can be carried out.

Decelerated Approach

A decelerated approach allows the aircraft to make a continuous descent towards the approach path which consumes less fuel than level offs and increased engine usage. The aircraft is assumed to be in the landing configuration at VAPP at 1000 ft.

Advantages of flying a decelerated approach are:

- Less emissions
- Less fuel consumption
- Less noise
- Saves time

Flap 3 Landing

The use of a Flap 3 landing will require a landing distance calculation in some cases, however the reductions in noise and fuel are worthwhile. The fuel reductions equate to roughly:

A319 - 16 kg saving

A320 - 9 kg saving

A321 - Flap 3 should not be used for cost saving

Arrival

Single engine taxi arrivals should be delayed until after 3 minutes from landing. This process also reduces brake wear from extended taxying on idle power from 2 engines and also will save on average around 18 kg of fuel (depending on the size of airport etc)

In general, there are many things that pilots can do to become more fuel efficient. These vary from carrying less fuel to single engine taxi and reduced APU usage.

However effective these measures may be, safety is always the priority so if you need to carry extra fuel as a precaution due to weather or slot delays then do it. The fuel savings on all of the other flights operated will still make a significant impact on the overall operation and fuel savings.

Fuel Usage

APU fuel burn	2 kg / min
Taxi fuel burn	10 kg / min OETD 7 kg / min
Holding (1500 ft)	40 kg / min
Approach Fuel	17 kg / min
Climb Phase	
ENG AI	+ 1.1 kg / min
ENG + WING AI	+ 2.0 kg / min
Cruise Phase	
ENG AI	+ 1.0 kg / min
ENG + WING AI	+ 2.0 kg / min
Holding Phase	
ENG AI	+ 2.0 kg / min
ENG + WING AI	+ 3.0 kg / min

Optimum Flight Level

The optimum flight level is based on a minimum time in the cruise of 5 minutes and at a minimum cruise level of FL100. It is the most economical flight level to be flown for the conditions specific to the flight.

This is calculated based on the gross weight of the aircraft, the wind, temperature and the cost index inserted. The resultant FL is a compromise between fuel burn and time saving and it can change in flight when the wind changes or when weight is reduced in the later stages of the cruise.

Recommended Max Flight Level

The A320 family is limited to FL398 which is the limitation for this field.

Based on the aircraft current gross weight and the temperature, the REC MAX indicates the max flight level to achieve the following:

- Level flight at Max CRZ thrust rating
- Speed greater than Green Dot and lower than VMO/MMO
- Maintain a VS of 300 ft/min at Max CLB thrust
- 0.3 g buffet margin

PERFORMANCE BASED NAVIGATION

PBN basically means navigating based on the performance requirements for the aircraft which is operating along a certain route, approach or airspace.

These requirements are expressed in navigation specifications in terms of integrity, accuracy, continuity and functionality needed for the proposed operation in a particular airspace. The availability of a GNSS signal should be available for these operations.

RNAV

RNAV (Area Navigation) allows aircraft to fly directly between two points, rather than flying directly overhead multiple radio beacons. This ensures a more direct routing and also allows operations where traditional VOR's are not available.

In 1993, the government allowed satellites to be used for commercial usage which now allows aircraft to use a GPS signal to confirm position. The aircraft needs to be within range of GPS reception and it can then navigate point to point.

To get an exact location, the GPS receiver must get a signal from 4 satellites simultaneously. When flying on a route between waypoints, the aircraft can now constantly update position, groundspeed, distance etc.

This GPS received information is used in conjunction with the aircrafts own Inertial Navigation system - IRS which calculate the flight path, altitude and attitude. As well as the GPS and IRS, the aircraft also uses VOR, DME and LOC signals. These additional sources allow the aircraft to have redundancy and the crew can still follow an arrival referring to traditional navigation aids if there is a failure of the GPS signal.

Required Navigation Performance - RNP

This allows aircraft the ability to fly directly between two 3D points in space. This now allows a 3D curved flight path to be flown which can be extremely efficient for mountainous terrain or congested airspace.

The main difference between RNAV and RNP is that RNP requires performance monitoring and alerting. In basic terms this means that the system is constantly checking itself to ensure its accuracy and navigation performance and will advise the pilots when it is not performing as expected.

Aircraft operating within RNP airspace should have a total position error equal to or less than the RNP value, achieved for 95% of the flight time.

RNP 1	Terminal Airspace	Nav ACCUR - 1.0 nm
RNP APCH	RNAV Final App	Nac ACCUR - 0.3 nm

The navigation source must be available at all times to conduct RNP Approaches. If the approach charts state that:

RNAV (GNSS) - GPS must be available for arrival

RNAV (VOR/DME) (DME/DME) VOR/ DME facilities must be available for use

PROCEDURES

Standard Takeoff Technique	259
Auto Flap Retract / Alpha Lock	260
Rejected Takeoff	261
Emergency Evacuation	262
Climb	263
Cruise	264
Descent Preparation	267
Descent	273
Approach	277
ILS Approach	284
RNAV Approach	289
Circling Approach	291
Visual Approach	292
Go Around / Baulked Landing	293
Windshear	294
PFD / ND Indications	297
Flight Mode Annunciator Modes	305

Takeoff Briefing

Weather	Wind direction, LVP's, RWY condition, anti-ice requirement
Aircraft	Defects, OEB's, CEO/NEO
NOTAMS	Departure, en-route, arrival
Threats	Terrain, MSA, Weather, any other relevant items for departure
Aircraft Status	Check correct aircraft, database valid, performance figure correct
INIT A	Routing, alternate,
F-PLN	Check departure SID, en-route, arrival STAR, distance, time
RAD NAV	Insert appropriate navaids
PROG	Check navigation accuracy for RNAV departures
PERF	Check V speeds, thrust reduction / acceleration if NADP1, speed restrictions for departure
FUEL PRED	Check trip time / fuel, block fuel, TOW, extra fuel
SEC F-PLN	STD / Non-STD EOSID
Questions	Ensure the other pilot is happy with your brief and fully understands the departure

Standard Takeoff Technique

If crosswind is at or below 20kts and no tailwind:	
Thrust levers	50% N1
Brakes	Release
Thrust Levers	FLX or TOGA
If crosswind is greater than 20kts or a tailwind:	
Brakes	Release
Thrust Levers	50% N1, check stabilised Increase thrust from 50% to 70% Above 15kts, increase to takeoff thrust by 40kts.
FMA	PF Reads FMA
100 kts	'Checked'
V1	Announce
'Rotate'	Rotate at around 3°/second towards 15° then follow SRS
'Positive Climb'	'Gear Up'
Above 100ft, either AP can be selected	
Thrust Reduction Alt - LVR CLB (Usually at 1000ft)	Reduce thrust levers to CLB detent - A/THR now becomes active
PACK 1 & 2	Pack 1 On Pack 2 On after 10 seconds
Acceleration Altitude	Speed change from V2 +10 to the first CLB speed
Flaps	Retract
Spoilers	Disarm
Landing lights	Off as required

**Above 130 kts, the connection between the nosewheel steering and the rudder pedals does not work. Use rudder to control the aircraft.*
**Release cabin crew by selecting seatbelt signs to OFF/ON to signal that they can commence duties. Done once flaps retracted incase there is an issue and a return is likely.*

Auto Flap Retract

This protection is required in some cases when the weight is heavy and there are speed restrictions to be met on the departure routing.

A319 / A320	210 kts
A321	215 kts / 225 kts
At the above speeds, the ARS will automatically retract the flaps to 0°. As the aircraft accelerates above S speed, the flap lever can be moved to 0. If the IAS decreases below VFE CONF1+F, the flaps will not extend back to 1+F.	

**It is good practice to select 230kts once you initiate the clean up phase. This ensures that you will not overspeed the flaps whilst they transition to the 0 position and the aircraft accelerates. Once clean, speed can be managed or selected to increase.*

Alpha Lock Protection

This protection prevents slat retraction at a high angle of attack of when low speed at the time the flap lever is moved from 1 to 0. A.LOCK will pulse on the E/WD. The protection is removed when the speed falls within a normal value, and the slats then retract. This occurs during heavy weight takeoff

If this occurs, continue acceleration to enable slat retraction and full clean up.

Rejected Takeoff

Before 100 kts	
Stop for any ECAM Warning / Caution	
Between 100 kts - V1	
Stop for Fire Warning / severe damage, loss of thrust, any red ECAM, amber cautions including: F/CTL SIDESTICK FAULT ENG FAIL ENG REVERSER FAULT ENG 1(2) THR LEVER FAULT ENG REVERSE UNLOCKED **Nose gear vibration should not be a reason to reject a takeoff*	
Above V1 - Takeoff must be continued	
Captain	**First Officer**
'STOP'	
Thrust Levers - Idle	
Reverse - Max	'Reverse Green'
	'Decel'
	Audio - Cancel
	ATC - Inform
	'70 kts' - Announce
Position the nose into wind to keep potential flames away from fuselage	
Reversers - Stow	
Parking Brake - Apply	Emer Evac checklist - Locate
'Attention, Crew at Stations' - PA	
'ECAM Actions'	Perform
If required at any time, ask for the emergency evacuation checklist	

**Announcing 'Decel' refers to a deceleration being felt by the crew.*
**DECEL light comes on when actual rate is 80% of selected decal rate*
**Autobrake & spoilers are inactive below 72 kts*
**After a complete stop using MAX autobrake, disarm spoilers to release brakes for taxi*

Emergency Evacuation

Captain	First Officer
'Emergency Evacuation checklist'	
'MAYDAY MAYDAY MAYDAY, ____ evacuating'	
'On'	'Parking Brake - Stop / On'
'Notified'	'ATC Notify'
'Alerted'	'Cabin Crew PA - Alert'
'Checked'	'Cabin Diff Pressure - N/A or zero'
	'ENG Masters - All OFF'
	'Fire Pushbuttons - Push'
Order agent discharge	'Agents - Discharge'
Evaluate the situation	'If Evacuation Required'
If Evacuation Required: PA for Evacuation Press EVAC COMMAND pb Evacuate	Evacuate

**Prior to turning off engines, turn DOME light On*
**Agents are not required unless positive signs of fire*

Climb

Managed	
Managed AP/FD vertical mode is CLB This is the only mode that will adhere to altitude constraints on the F-PLN Only available in NAV mode Managed speed is computed by the FMGS This is computed using weight, winds, ISA deviation and cost index. Managed speed adheres to speed restrictions on departures.	
Selected	
OP CLB	Used when in HDG mode Maintains speed target but not altitude restrictions within the F-PLN Often results in high vertical climb rates which can be a threat in congested airspace
V/S	Used to specify a given climb rate Recommended to be used for small altitude changes which results in smoother thrust variations V/S is not recommended for normal vertical profile commands, if a high V/S is selected, the aircraft may not be able to climb due to performance reasons, resulting is the speed reducing to VLS. At this point the AP will force a pitch down command Warning - V/S takes precedence over speed
EXPED	Used to increase vertical speed to a specific level Selects Green Dot in Climb for max gradient Selects M 0.80 / 340 kts in descent Should be avoided above FL250
- Selected speed to achieve ***max rate of climb*** (in the shortest time) is between ECON CLB speed and green dot. Turbulence penetration speed can be used for this. - Selected speed to achieve **max gradient of climb** (shortest distance) is Green Dot. It is possible to fly below green dot speed but this has no operational benefit and could be a threat.	

Cruise

PROG page will display the cruise level selected. If ATC advise that the current level is final and it is below the selected level, press any number or letter, then select L1 on the MCDU whilst in PROG page and the current level will become ALT CRZ

This is more beneficial for longer cruise as ALT CRZ will automatically select the cruise Mach number (if in managed speed) which will usually be different from the climb speed or intermediate level off speed.

When flying at the cruise FL, AP will allow a small altitude variation of around +/- 50 ft to maintain the Mach number, resulting in fewer thrust changes, thus improving fuel efficiency. This is called 'soft mode'.

Cost Index

This is the relationship between the time and fuel and aims to minimize the cost of the flight. This figure is usually displayed on flight plans and is specific to each airline operator on the number given for a certain route pairing. CI is used to help reduce direct operating costs

The CI is expressed in kilograms per min (kg/min) or as hundreds of pounds per hour (100 lbs/hr)

Cost Index affects speed and cruise altitude.

CI 0   Equals maximum range
CI 999 Equals minimum time

Cruise Speed

Managed Speed
A/THR operates in SPEED or MACH mode when at cruise level The optimum cruise speed depends on CI, temperature, cruise level, weight and any headwind. Increasing headwind of 1 kt will equate to a M 0.01 increase To achieve a specific time over a waypoint, a vertical revision to the waypoint can be made with a time constraint. MACH will then be modified to achieve this, a magenta * will appear on the MCDU if this can be met, an amber * will show if not.

Selected Speed
Selected speed in the cruise is generally only used if required from ATC or if there is turbulence present. This speed should never be less than greet dot at higher altitudes, as the aircraft may not be able to maintain altitude or speed. The increased drag due to the aircrafts profile may be more than the available thrust available.

Turbulence Penetration Speed

Altitude	*A319*	*A320 CEO*	*A320 NEO*	*A321 NEO*
0 - 20,000	250 kts	250 kts	260 kts	275 kts
20,000 - 32,000	275 kts	275 kts	280 kts	305 kts*
Above 32,000	M 0.76	M 0.76	M 0.76	M 0.76

*A321 NEO - 305kts applies to altitude range 20,000ft - 27,000ft

REC MAX FL

This figure is a representation of the engine and wing performance and provides a 0.3 g buffet margin, minimum rate of climb in max CLB thrust and to maintain level flight at max CRZ thrust. The maximum flight level is FL398.

If a higher FL is entered in the PROG page which results in a buffet margin of less than 0.2 g, then the message CRZ ABOVE MAX FL will show.

This altitude is calculated based on weight and temperature and assumes anti-ice is off.

The REX MAX FL should always be the upper cruise limit for the aircraft, above this leads to the threat of reduced performance margins, large speed deviations or turbulence and subsequently an upset or stall situation.

OPT FL

This shows the cruise altitude for minimum cost when managed ECON speed is being flown and should be used where possible. This is only accurate when the wind and temperature has been entered correctly, and also uses information from gross weight and the cost index.

A cruise of 5 minutes at a minimum FL100 is required.

Fuel Temperature Checks

JET A1	*A319*	*A320 CEO*	*A320 NEO*	*A321 NEO*
MIN	*-43 ℃*	*-43 ℃*	*-43 ℃*	*-43 ℃*
MAX	*54 ℃*	*54 ℃*	*55 ℃*	*55 ℃*
Min environmental conditions -70 ℃				

Descent Preparation

Preparation for the arrival should have been pre planned so the main requirement is to check the weather is suitable for arrival time, NOTAMs are reviewed and the landing distance calculation (if required) has been completed.

Generally, the crew will have checked at dispatch that the planned conditions will be acceptable, and the factored landing distance (FLD) will be less than the landing distance available (LDA).

DISPATCH LDG PERF
This is used to determine the max allowed landing weight and is used for pre-flight planning. It is assessed using the weather conditions as well as the runway surface at the expected landing time.
IN-FLIGHT LDG PERF
This is used to determine the factored landing distance which will then be used to assess the margin for the landing distance available. This is based on reported conditions at the landing airport. Using this information, pilots can assess the use of the following: • Flap Configuration (CONF 3 or CONF FULL) • Braking Mode LOW / MED / Manual • Thrust Reverse (IDLE / MAX)

Pilots should assess landing performance using two steps:

- Use an RCAM (Runway Condition Assessment Matrix) table to assess the braking performance level
- Use the QRH Perf section or a landing performance software application. Both of these should include a 15% safety margin to the landing distance - known as the *Factored* in flight landing distance.

RCAM Table

<table>
<tr><th colspan="2">Runway Surface Conditions</th><th rowspan="2">Observations on Deceleration and Directional Control</th><th colspan="2">Related Landing Performance</th><th rowspan="2">Maximum Crosswind (Gust included)</th></tr>
<tr><th>Runway State or / and Runway Contaminant</th><th>ESF* or PIREP**</th><th>Code</th><th>Level</th></tr>
<tr><td>Dry</td><td>-</td><td>-</td><td>6</td><td>DRY</td><td>38kt</td></tr>
<tr><td>Damp
Wet
Up to 3 mm (1/8") of water</td><td rowspan="2">Good</td><td rowspan="2">Braking deceleration is normal for the wheel braking effort applied. Directional control is normal.</td><td rowspan="2">5</td><td rowspan="2">GOOD</td><td>38kt</td></tr>
<tr><td>Slush
Up to 3 mm (1/8")
Dry snow
Up to 3 mm (1/8")
Wet snow
Up to 3 mm (1/8")
Frost</td><td>29kt</td></tr>
<tr><td>Compacted Snow
OAT at or below -15°C</td><td>Good to Medium</td><td>Braking deceleration and controllability is between Good and Medium.</td><td>4</td><td>GOOD TO MEDIUM</td><td>29kt</td></tr>
<tr><td>Dry Snow
More than 3 mm (1/8"), up to 100 mm (4")
Wet Snow
More than 3 mm (1/8"), up to 30 mm (6/5")
Compacted Snow
OAT above -15°C
Slippery when wet</td><td>Medium</td><td>Braking deceleration is noticeably reduced for the wheel braking effort applied. Directional control may be reduced.</td><td>3</td><td>MEDIUM</td><td>25kt</td></tr>
<tr><td>Water
More than 3 mm (1/8"), up to 12.7 mm (1/2")
Slush
More than 3 mm (1/8"), up to 12.7 mm (1/2")</td><td>Medium to Poor</td><td>Braking deceleration and controllability is between Medium and Poor. Potential for Hydroplaning exists.</td><td>2</td><td>MEDIUM TO POOR</td><td>20kt</td></tr>
<tr><td>Ice (cold & dry)</td><td>Poor</td><td>Braking deceleration is significantly reduced for the wheel braking effort applied. Directional control may be significantly reduced.</td><td>1</td><td>POOR</td><td>15kt</td></tr>
<tr><td>Wet ice
Water on top of Compacted Snow
Dry Snow or Wet Snow over ice</td><td>Nil</td><td>Braking deceleration is minimal to non-existent for the wheel braking effort applied. Directional control may be uncertain.</td><td>-</td><td>-</td><td>-</td></tr>
</table>

**ESF: Estimated Surface Friction*
***PIREP: Pilot Report of Braking Action*

How to use the RCAM table:

- Each runway condition is grouped into a different Runway Condition Code (RWYCC). This is based on the deceleration and directional control of the aircraft.
- The RWY CC will be allocated to each 1/3 of the runway
- Information on the runway surface should be sourced from ATIS / METAR / SNOWTAM / ATC / NOTAM etc.
- Crew will then review this information to make an assessment on the runway condition - this is called the Primary braking performance level.
- The crew may decide to downgrade this level if Pilot Report of Braking Action (PiREP) is available and concludes a lower braking level, SNOWTAM indicates a lower level or any other information relates to a degradation of performance

**Under no circumstances should the crew upgrade the performance level.*

Global Reporting Format

ICAO have recently adopted a new way for airports to report the runway surface condition and this is known as the Global Reporting Format (GRF). When runway conditions are not Dry, a Runway Condition Report (RCR) must be provided with the following information:

- Runway Condition Code (RWYCC)
- Type of contamination
- Depth and coverage for each 1/3 of runway from threshold onwards.

This reporting system means that RCAM tables are more frequently used for crosswind landing assessments. If the RCR does not contain information on the RWYCC, crew can use the RCAM table to determine this.

VAPP considerations

The approach speed or VAPP should always be considered as part of any approach. It is calculated using aircraft weight, flap/slat configuration, winds, ice and A/THR use.

Generally the FMGC will calculate the VAPP speed and displays this in the PERF page. If no A/THR is used this can be lowered to VLS but generally the VAPP should be at least VLS + 5 kts in conditions of gusty winds above 20 kts. This can be increased to a maximum of VLS + 15 kts.

VAPP is computed using the estimated landing weight whilst in the CRZ or DES phase of flight. Once the Approach phase is selected, VAPP is calculated using the current gross weight - bear this in mind for extended arrivals or reduced track miles.

Generally managed speed should always be used for approaches unless strong winds dictate that a selected speed would be more beneficial.

VAPP = VLS + APPR COR

VAPP with a failure

Some failures including flaps or slats issues will increase the VLS, others will require a higher approach speed to be flown due to handling characteristics of the aircraft. This speed will need to be added to VLS to give an Approach speed.

Airbus recommends that this increase should not be above 20 kts as this directly affects the landing distance.

VAPP with a failure is calculated using the reference speed (VREF) which is VLS in CONF Full, and also the effect of the failure on the reference speed (ΔVREF), plus the approach correction (APPR COR)

VAPP = VREF + ΔVREF + APPR COR

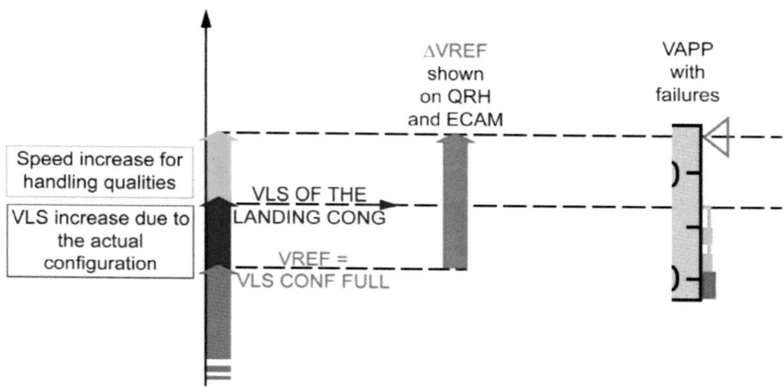

Missed Approach Climb Gradient

Generally published for specific approaches and sometimes specific minima. A minimum gradient of 2.5% is required and if different, this will be published.

Go Around Climb Gradient

The GA gradient is always computed at 1500 ft. This is affected by altitude, outside air temperature and QNH.

One Engine inop Go Around Altitude

The aircraft needs to accelerate in level flight to retract the flaps. Crew must establish the minimum one engine inop acceleration altitude based on:

- Default of 1500 ft
- Missed Approach Level Acceleration Altitude
- Minimum Flight Altitude on missed approach procedure
- Initial Go Around Altitude

Flap Setting Selection

A319 / A320	
Flap Full	**Flap 3**
Used if tailwind greater than 10 kts	If windshear / turbulence is predicted on approach Improves go-around performance
CONF3 reduces noise on approach and saves fuel *No runway contamination should be present*	
A321	
Flap Full	**Flap 3**
Standard for normal Operations	If windshear / turbulence is predicted on approach Improves go-around performance
Recommended to increase VAPP to VLS + 10 kts to reduce tail strike risk	

If Flap 3 is required, select GPWS LDG FLAP 3 pb switch to ON and select FLAP 3 on the PERF page on the MCDU.

Thrust Reverse

DISPATCH Computation	
Dry	All Reversers inoperative
Wet	All Reversers inoperative
Contaminated	All Reversers operative*

**Crew to select thrust reverser status as MEL item to deselect for contaminated runway.*

IN-FLIGHT Computation		
DRY	RWYCC 6	Select REV IDLE on landing Thrust Reverse credit: REV no (STD)
WET	RWYCC 5	Select REV IDLE. Perform calc based on: RWY COND - 3 - MEDIUM AUTOBRAKE LOW or MED REV set to No (STD) No Reverser Credit
Contaminated	RWYCC <4	Thrust Reverser credit: REV Yes Select REV MAX on landing

Descent

Descent is initiated using either managed descent mode (DES) or selected descent modes (OP DES, V/S). Either modes can be flown with either managed or selected speed modes, however DES mode can be used in conjunction with NAV only.

Managed Descent
The descent profile is generally around 2.5° Priority is given to the vertical descent profile, if speed increases with engines at idle power, speedbrakes will be required to reduce speed. In extreme situations the AP will prevent speed from exceeding VMO/MMO. If DECELERATE or T/D REACHED appears on the PFD, reduce speed to green dot until descent clearance has been given. Speed in managed mode will have a range to allow the vertical profile to be maintained, in some cases the upper speed range can be close to VMO/MMO, in this case it may be wise to use OPEN DES until the speed window has a large enough buffer, then resume managed speed. Aircraft on descent path: • Speed margins not displayed • Elevators adjust pitch to maintain profile • MORE DRAG should not be displayed • Half speedbrakes may be required to maintain profile Aircraft above descent path: • Descent rate increases to maintain vertical profile • Speed increases to upper speed range limit • Idle thrust commanded • If a constraint is predicted to be missed, MORE DRAG will show on the PFD

Selected Descent

Open Descent and V/S are the two speeds used for a selected descent.

When open descent is used, the A/THR commands idle thrust and the speed is controlled by the THS. There is no speed range target as there is no vertical profile to achieve.

Any constraints in the vertical profile will not be met and an unrestricted descent will be flown to the altitude selected in the FCU window.

Open descent and speedbrake is very effective if high on the descent profile however car should be taken as the VLS will increase with speedbrake use so monitor the speed on the PFD carefully.

V/S is used for a specific or more shallow descent rate. SPEED mode activates and in this configuration, speedbrakes should not be used as thrust will likely already be applied, working against the speedbrakes.

Expedite Descent

Pushing the EXPED pb on the FCU adjusts the target speed to become either M 0.8 or 340 kts, whichever is lower.

FMA displays THR IDLE / EXP DES / NAV

- To return to DES mode, push FCU ALT knob
- To return to OP DES mode, pull SPD or ALT
- To return to SPEED / VS mode, pull FCU V/S knob

Due to the high speeds and descent rates, it is extremely important to monitor the speed, speed trend and the FMA's.

Descent Management

The aim of good descent management is to have the aircraft adhere to all speed / altitude restraints on the descent path, and to be stable once commencing the approach.

The first stage of this is the Top of Descent (TOD) point. This is calculated through the FMGS, based on pilot inputs. It is a good idea to ensure that the winds have been updated for descent, also check the track miles that you expect to fly. Some arrivals are often shortened so bear this in mind and adjust altitude / speed constraints accordingly.

- Modify routing to be representative of the expected arrival routing
- Use route discontinuities
- Adjust altitude / speed constraints
- Use the Secondary Flight Plan to plan for any runway change or a longer routing

A 'guide' to calculate miles required for descent is using the following:

Track miles required	Height x 3 (E.g. 8000ft 8 x 3 = 24nm) + 1 nm per 10 kts for speed deceleration +/- 1 nm per 10 kts tailwind / headwind

A regular check of the above will enable more accurate descent management and is a good cross check for both pilots.

The distance to the runway can be found using the PROG page and entering the runway threshold, or slightly more accurate is by using a co-located ILS with DME (displayed on the PFD).

If the FMGC is accurate, start the descent in DES mode. The aircraft will then adhere to constraints and restrictions. If ATC ask you to amend the descent, then it may be required to use either OPEN DES to increase descent rate or use V/S to shallow the descent rate.

It is important to ensure the flightplan is correctly sequenced and the waypoint in white at the top right of the ND is the one ahead of the aircraft. If ATC have taken you off the arrival routing via a heading, ensure that waypoints behind the aircraft are cleared from the route.

If low on profile:
Use V/S to reduce the descent rate until the profile can be re-captured
If high on profile:
Speedbrakes can be used to increase descent rate without increasing speed if under a constraint. The lower the speed, the less efficient the speedbrake. To achieve the maximum descent rate, use speedbrakes and OPEN DES with a higher selected speed. *MAX Speedbrake with AP engaged is only Half speedbrake. Moving the speedbrake handle to full will not give full deployment* *Disengaging the AP will allow for full speedbrake deployment.* *(Not Applicable to A319)*

Ensure suitable speeds are adhered to whilst turning - the turn radius is much greater at high speed.

If necessary, ask ATC for more track miles to prepare for the approach. Always monitor the descent against the arrival chart, make adjustments early and ensure the aircraft is in a stable configuration to enable flap extension in preparation for the final approach.

Approach

Generally the approach is divided into 3 segments - initial approach, intermediate approach and the final approach. Whilst there are certain tasks that need to be carried out for each, much of these should be established during the brief enabling both pilots to already anticipate how the aircraft will be flown and allowing both to monitor the flight path and ensure a safe landing is always established.

Initial Approach

Flight plan sequencing should always be checked to ensure that the TO waypoint on the upper ND is correct and is a waypoint in front of the aircraft, this should be automatically done whilst in NAV mode. If using HDG or TRK, the flight plan will sequence when the aircraft is close to the planned route to be flown, however this can cause issues if you overfly an airport as it will assume you are at a waypoint possibly on the final approach and even will erase the flight plan. A good tip here is to use the secondary flight plan and copy the active if not required, or you can use the DIR TO RADIAL IN function - always 180° difference from the landing inbound runway heading.

Activate the Approach Phase - This allows the aircraft to decelerate to VAPP speed or any inserted speed constraints entered at the Final Descent Point.

In HDG mode this will need to be done manually via the PERF page on the MCDU. If this is not done then when the pilot pushes to manage the speed to decelerate further for flap selection, the last managed speed will be selected which could cause a large thrust increase and risk an unstable approach.

In NAV mode, the approach phase will automatically activate at the assigned deceleration waypoint. This can still be done manually by the pilots if an earlier deceleration is required.

Intermediate Approach

This segment of the approach is aimed at decelerating the aircraft to an appropriate speed and configuration to be established at the Final Descent Point (FDP).

In most approaches, managed speed should always be used. When the approach phase has been activated, the A/THR will reduce speed to the maneuvering speed of the current flap setting. To reduce additional thrust changes, it is good practice to select the next flap setting when the speed is reducing to the current maneuvering speed +10kts. This deceleration rate will be approximately 10 kts / NM whilst level.

If using a selected speed, this can be below the maneuvering speed of the current flap setting, however never below VLS. When the selected speed is no longer required and further deceleration needed, managed speed can again be pushed on the FCU.

If the aircraft is fast on the approach, the crew can either use the landing gear or speed brakes to aid the deceleration.

The landing gear is very effective as it causes huge amounts of drag which will allow the speed to settle even with tailwinds or steep approaches. The speed brakes should be used with caution - an increase in VLS should be anticipated and also they become less effective at lower speeds.

Decelerated Approach

It is often heard in a brief that a 'Standard' decelerated approach will be carried out. There is no 'standard' to this approach type as it refers to the aircraft being in the landing configuration, at VAPP at 1000 ft.

In order to achieve this however the pilots may wish to slow down earlier due to a slightly steeper glide path angle, closing distance reducing to the proceeding aircraft or if the cabin is not secure. This means that generally the approach prior to this point can be flown in various configurations, however at 1000 ft, the aircraft must be in the landing configuration and speed at VAPP. This means that at the Final Descent Point, the aircraft is in CONF 1 and at S Speed.

Stabilised Approach

A stabilised approach is commonly used where the aircraft has had a failure, for certain non-precision approaches or if the glideslope is very steep. The aircraft should be at the Final Descent Point in the landing configuration and at VAPP. It is expected that the pilots enter VAPP at the Final Descent Point, however the speed will already be controlled by the selection of flaps down to the landing configuration.

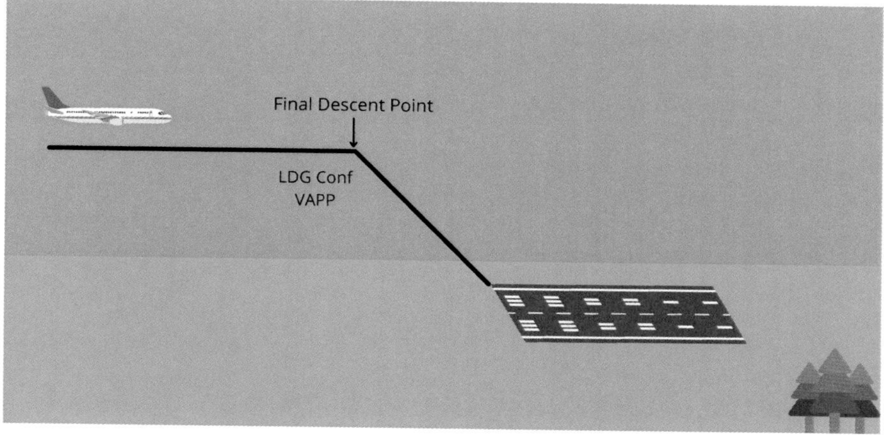

Stability Criteria

All approaches should be stable by 1000 ft and must be stable by 500 ft.

Stable Criteria	
Aircraft in Landing Configuration	
On correct Lateral and Vertical flight path (reference to G/S, PAPI)	
Bank Angle - Maximum 15°	
Final Approach Speed + 10 / - 5 kts	
Go Around if:	
By 1000 ft RA	Not in the landing Configuration
	Speed more than VAPP + 30 kts
By 500 ft RA	Stable Approach criteria not met
	Landing checklist not complete

It is not necessary for the Pilot monitoring to call out deviations due to atmospheric conditions / wind changes.

The 1000 ft reference may not be suitable for use at airports where terrain is changing. In these situations, this reference should be to the TDZE.

Circling Approach Stability Criteria - 400 ft
Aircraft in landing configuration
Landing checklist completed
On correct lateral and vertical flight path (reference to G/S, PAPI)
Final Approach Speed + 10 / - 5 kts
Bank Angle Max 15° within +/- 30° of final track

Discontinued Approach

A discontinued approach is carried out when the aircraft is above the FCU selected altitude. A standard Go Around could be carried out, however the discontinued approach allows for a less extreme and more comfortable procedure. This does not require the crew to select TOGA.

At or above the FCU altitude:

- Pilot calls 'Cancel Approach'
- Press APPR pb or LOC pb to disarm AP/FD approach mode
- Select either NAV or HDG lateral mode
- Select suitable V/S or level off
- Select a suitable speed

If the Flight plan has been lost, insert a new lateral revision or in the NEW DEST field. There will usually be a published go around procedure – this can be confirmed with ATC.

The aircraft will remain in the Approach phase as the thrust levers are not moved into the TOGA detent.

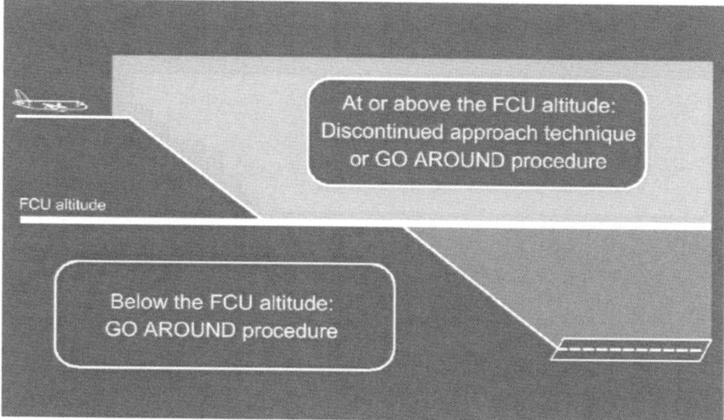

Go Around

The last point at which a pilot can initiate a go around is the selection of reverse thrust. Close to the ground, pilots should anticipate the effect of the TOGA thrust and try to avoid large rotation rates which could lead to a tail strike. Due to the spool up time from the by-pass engine and low thrust setting, a height loss should be expected initially.

The landing gear could come into contact with the ground, if this occurs the pilots should still anticipate a normal go around to follow.

If the aircraft is on the runway when TOGA is applied, the red ECAM warning CONFIG may occur - pilots should disregard this.

Procedure:	
Thrust Levers	TOGA
	TOGA then FLX/MCT if equipped with soft GA
Rotation	Monitor if AP on
	15° is no AP
	12.5° if single engine

The speed in the go around will be the highest of VAPP or IAS at TOGA selection. This is limited to VLS + 25kts with both engines and VLS + 15 kts with one engine inop. At the acceleration altitude, the target speed becomes green dot.

If the flight plan is sequenced, the missed approach routing should automatically be shown on the ND and if available, NAV mode will engage to follow this.

If extended, the Speedbrakes automatically retract.

Glideslope Intercept from Above

If the aircraft is high on the approach and above the glideslope, use the following technique to capture:

APPR pb	Push to arm APPR (G/S Blue
V/S	Set -1500 ft initially
FCU Altitude	Set above aircraft altitude*
When G/S engages	Set Go Around altitude in FCU

*DO NOT PULL the ALT selector knob on the FCU when selecting a higher altitude - this will engage OP CLB and may result in a Go Around.

A good configuration is Flap 2, Gear down and 180 kts selected to ensure sufficient drag. Speed brakes may be used but monitor VLS increase when doing so.

V/S greater than -2000 fpm may result in speed increasing towards VFE

V/S mode ensures the autothrust is in SPEED mode and not THR IDLE

Aircraft should be stable by 1000 ft and must be stable by 500 ft - if not then a Go Around must be flown.

<table>
<tr><td colspan="4">CAT I ILS Approach</td></tr>
<tr><td>Decision Height</td><td colspan="3">200 ft</td></tr>
<tr><td>RVR Required</td><td>550 m</td><td>125 m (if reported)</td><td>75 m (If reported)</td></tr>
<tr><td>FMA Displayed</td><td colspan="3">CAT I</td></tr>
<tr><td>Lighting Required</td><td colspan="3">Any elements of approach lighting</td></tr>
<tr><td>Autoland</td><td colspan="3">Possible - Care must be taken as ILS unprotected</td></tr>
<tr><td colspan="4">When CAT 1 Displayed on FMA - Autopilot available until - 160 ft</td></tr>
<tr><td colspan="4">When cleared for the ILS, push the APPR pb. This will arm the LOC and GS modes, which should be checked in blue on the FMA. Do this when:

• Cleared for the approach
• On the intercept trajectory for final approach course
• Within LOC capture envelope

Select the second AP, this offers redundancy.</td></tr>
<tr><td>Above 5000 ft</td><td colspan="3">FMA displays CAT 1</td></tr>
<tr><td>Below 5000 ft</td><td colspan="3">FMA displays intended approach capability</td></tr>
</table>

<table>
<tr><th colspan="4">LTS CAT I ILS Approach</th></tr>
<tr><td>Decision Height</td><td colspan="3">200 ft</td></tr>
<tr><td>RVR Required</td><td>400 m</td><td>125 m (if reported)</td><td>75 m (If reported)</td></tr>
<tr><td>FMA</td><td colspan="3">CAT 2 CAT 3 SINGLE CAT 3 DUAL</td></tr>
<tr><td>Lighting Required</td><td colspan="3">3 consecutive lights, any lateral light</td></tr>
<tr><td>Autoland</td><td colspan="3">Mandatory in most cases</td></tr>
<tr><td colspan="4">When CAT 1 Displayed on FMA - Autopilot available until - 160 ft</td></tr>
<tr><td colspan="4">LTS CAT I allows for a lower RVR minima to be flown for a CAT I ILS approach.
• LVP's must be in force
• LTS CAT I minima published for intended ILS approach
• At least 1 AP coupled for the approach and automatic landing
• Nothing prohibiting LTS CAT I</td></tr>
<tr><td>Above 5000 ft</td><td colspan="3">FMA displays CAT 1</td></tr>
<tr><td>Below 5000 ft</td><td colspan="3">FMA displays intended approach capability</td></tr>
</table>

CAT II ILS Approach			
Decision Height	**100 ft**		
RVR Required	**300 m**	**125 m**	**75 m**
FMA	CAT 2 CAT 3 SINGLE CAT 3 DUAL		
Lighting Required	3 consecutive lights, any lateral light		
Autoland	Mandatory		
When CAT 2 Displayed on FMA - Autopilot available until - 0 ft			
• LVP's must be in force • At least 1 AP coupled for the approach and automatic landing • For manual landing, AP disconnected by 80 ft to ensure a smooth transition to manual landing			
Above 5000 ft	FMA displays CAT 1		
Below 5000 ft	FMA displays intended approach capability		

<table>
<tr><th colspan="4">CAT III A ILS Approach</th></tr>
<tr><td>Decision Height</td><td colspan="3">100 ft - 50 ft</td></tr>
<tr><td>RVR Required</td><td>200 m</td><td>125 m</td><td>75 m</td></tr>
<tr><td>FMA</td><td colspan="3">CAT 3 SINGLE CAT 3 DUAL</td></tr>
<tr><td>Lighting Required</td><td colspan="3">3 consecutive lights</td></tr>
<tr><td>Autoland</td><td colspan="3">Mandatory</td></tr>
<tr><td colspan="4">When CAT 3 SINGLE Displayed on FMA - Autopilot available until - 0 ft</td></tr>
<tr><td colspan="4">CAT III SINGLE is when the systems are fail passive. This means that a single failure will lead to AP disconnection without any significant out of trim condition or deviation from flight path or attitude. Manual flight will then be required.

• LVP's must be in force
• At least 1 AP coupled for the approach and automatic landing
• Minimum decision height is 50 ft</td></tr>
<tr><td>Above 5000 ft</td><td colspan="3">FMA displays CAT 1</td></tr>
<tr><td>Below 5000 ft</td><td colspan="3">FMA displays intended approach capability</td></tr>
</table>

CAT III B ILS Approach			
Decision Height	**0 ft**		
RVR Required	**75 m**	**75 m**	**75 m**
FMA	CAT 3 DUAL		
Lighting Required	1 centreline light if a DH is used		
Autoland	Mandatory		
When CAT 3 DUAL Displayed on FMA - Autopilot available until - 0 ft			
CAT III DUAL is displayed when systems are fail operational. In case of a single failure, AP will continue to guide the aircraft on the flight path and the automatic landing system will operate as a fail passive system. Any failure below the alert height will mean that the approach, flare and landing will be completed normally by the remaining part of the automatic system. This redundancy allows CAT III ops with or without a DH. • LVP's must be in force • Both AP's coupled for the approach and automatic landing			
Above 5000 ft	FMA displays CAT 1		
Below 5000 ft	FMA displays intended approach capability		

FINAL APP Approach

Final App used for:

- RNP Approach using LNAV or LNAV/VNAV minima
- FINAL APP guidance for conventional VOR/NDB approach

Always check the minimum temperature on the approach chart

Aircraft minimum equipment required for an RNP Approach:

- One FMGC
- One GPS
- Two IRS
- One MCDU
- One FD
- One PFD on PF side
- Two ND's
- Two FCU channels

Degraded Navigation

RNP Approaches using LNAV minima

Use the remaining AP/FD if the following occur:

- GPS PRIMARY LOST on one ND
- NAV ACCUR DOWNGRAD on one FMGS

Discontinue approach in the following cases if not visual:

- GPS PRIMARY LOST on both ND's
- XTK > 0.3 nm
- NAV FM/GPS POS DISAGREE on the ECAM
- NAV ACCUR DOWNGRAD on both FMGS

FINAL APP Descent Preparation	
Weather	Low Outside Air Temperature is not accounted for using the vertical profile. Managed vertical guidance not to be used when OAT is below min temperature on approach chart
F-PLN Page	0.1° difference between MCDU and vertical path on the chart is fine Check the F-PLN from the navigation database against the chart. Tracks and distances should be correctly shown on the ND
PROG Page	Enter the landing runway threshold a BRG/DST to monitor the approach
Go Around	This should be briefed to include the management of downgraded / failed equipment

Flying The Approach	
APPR pb on FCU	Press when cleared for approach and when TO waypoint is the Final Descent Point. **Or when on level segment at final descent altitude and FDP sequenced correctly*
APP NAV / FINAL	Check armed / engaged
Flight Parameters - Monitor	PM to call excessive deviation XTK > 0.1 nn V/DEV > ½ Dot
One Hundred Above Minimum	Monitor / Announce
Minimum	Monitor / Announce
If Visual	Continue AP - OFF (250 ft latest) FD - As Required for use
If not Visual	Go Around

Circling Approach

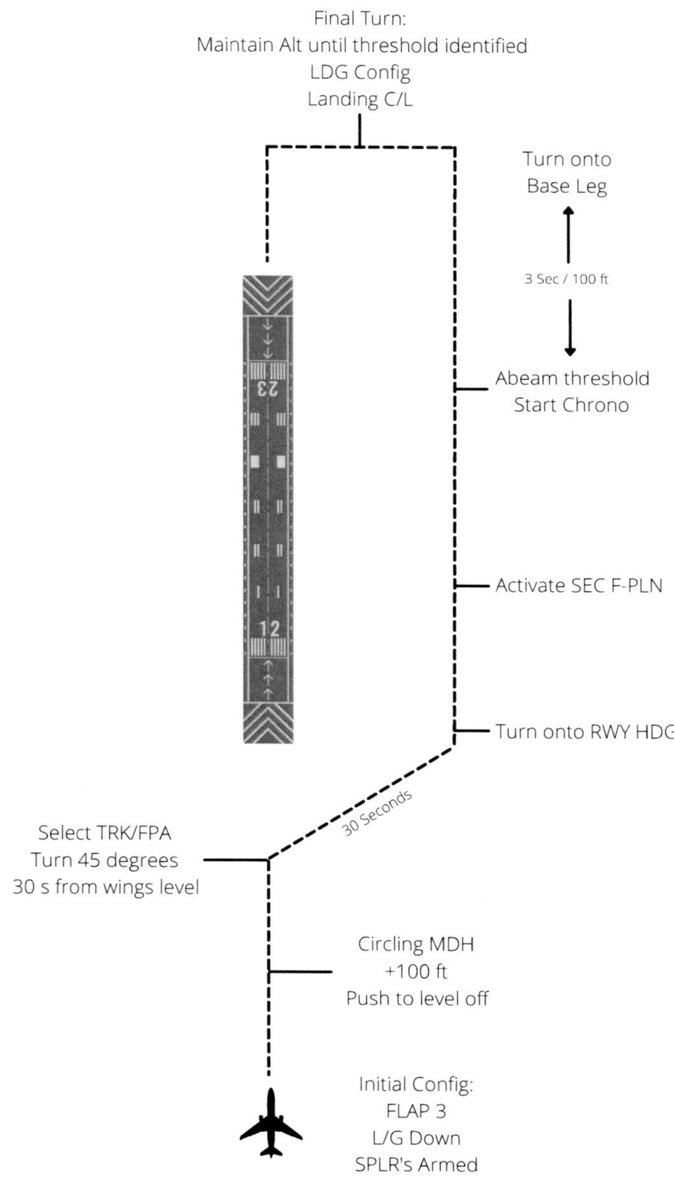

Visual Approach

Visual approaches can be performed for a variety of reasons such as traditional approach aids are not available or crews wanting to practice hand flying skills on a fair weather day.

Most commonly, the standard 3° glideslope should be flown. If there is an operational ILS on the landing runway, this should be selected in the FMGC and the LS pb selected. Crews can then monitor the approach and this also allows the GPWS to provide auto calls for G/S deviation.

Initial Approach	
APPR Phase	Activate
AP / FD	OFF
A/THR	ON / Managed Speed
TRK-FPA	Select
Extend downwind leg to 45 seconds +/- 1 s per kt of headwind or tailwind, for a standard 1500 ft circuit.	
Final Approach	
Flap 2	
Gear Down	
Flap 3	
Flap FULL	
Ensure Spoilers Armed	
Stable by 500 ft	

Go Around	
PM will simultaneously:	
Thrust Levers	TOGA *TOGA then FLEX for a/c with SOFT GA*
Rotate	Towards 15° *Avoid excessive rotation rates to avoid tailstrike*
Go Around	Announce
Flaps	Retract one stage
FMA	Announce
Positive Climb	Announce
Landing Gear	UP
Lateral Navigation	Select HDG or NAV
AP	Engage
**If AP engaged, monitor rotation rate, take over if needed*	

Baulked Landing	
'I Have Control'	Announce - Press and hold red takeover pb on sidestick
Thrust Levers	TOGA
Pitch	Adjust *May require holding altitude or de-rotating to achieve correct pitch*
Go Around	Announce *When safely climbing away from the ground, 'Go Around Flap' is announced and the standard go around procedure can be followed.* *If* CONFIG FLAPS NOT IN TO CONFIG *appears on ECAM, crew can disregard*

Windshear

Windshear is usually associated with the following situations:

- Strong Winds
- Jet Streams
- Mountain Waves
- Thunderstorms and Convective Clouds
- Microbursts

How this affects the Aircraft:

- Headwind gusts increase the aircraft speed and potentially make the aircraft fly above the intended path, or accelerate.
- Tailwind gusts decrease the aircraft speed and potentially makes the aircraft fly below the intended path, or decelerate.
- Downdrafts affect the Angle of Attack (AofA) which increases, and the aircraft induces a sink.

Indications of possible Windshear:

- Ground Speed Variations
- Indicated airspeed variations in excess of 15 kt
- Vertical Speed changes of 500 ft / min
- Wind variations in direction / velocity
- Excessive Pitch changes of 5° or more
- Heading variations of 10°
- Glideslope deviation of 1 dot
- Unusual A/THR activity or thrust lever position

The SPEED SPEED SPEED Low energy warning is based on the aircraft speed, acceleration and flight path angle. This will generally be the first warning to appear before the activation of alpha floor.

Reactive Windshear

Flight Augmentation Computers (FAC) generate the information using Angle of Attack data to determine instantaneous windshear, giving ECAM warnings. If windshear is detected by this system or by pilot observation, the recovery procedure must be applied.

Predictive Windshear

Information is produced from the weather radar which interrogates the Doppler shift in water droplets in order to map out areas of likely windshear ahead of the aircraft and produces advisories, cautions and warnings.

This remains on even if the weather radar is switched off, provided the windshear switch on the weather radar is set to AUTO. Atmospheric moisture must be present for this system to be effective.

The three tools used to assist pilots to escape from Windshear are:

Alpha Floor Protection	A/THR Commands TOGA on both engines FMA displays A.FLOOR, changing to TOGA.LK when AofA has decreased. This can be deselected by turning the A/THR off
SRS AP/FD Pitch Law	Ensures best climb performance - follow SRS orders to minimize height loss
High AofA Protection	Enables PF to pull full aft on sidestick. Provides maximum lift and minimum drag. Automatically retracts speedbrakes if extended

	Reactive	Predictive		
Level	Warning	Warning	Caution	Advisory
PFD	**WINDSHEAR (min 15s)**	**W/S AHEAD**	W/S AHEAD	Nil
Aural	"Windshear, windshear, windshear" (only once)	Takeoff: "Windshear ahead, windshear ahead" Landing: "Go around, windshear ahead"	"Monitor radar display"	Nil
PF Actions	Apply TOGA Call "Windshear TOGA" Follow SRS orders* (keep A/P if engaged) DO NOT change aircraft configuration until out of windshear (Red Windshear on PFD removed) Monitor flight path and speed. Recover smoothly to normal climb when out of windshear.	Takeoff: Reject takeoff Airborne: Apply TOGA Follow SRS orders* (keep A/P if engaged), turn to avoid windshear symbol Landing: Go around, perform.* You CAN change the aircraft configuration if not in windshear	Before takeoff: Delay takeoff. Select the most favourable runway considering likely windshear. Use TOGA thrust and monitor the airspeed and trends during takeoff run for early signs of windshear During approach: Delay landing until conditions improve, or divert. Select the most favourable runway. Use Config 3 and managed speed in the approach phase. Increase VAPP up to VLS+15kt. Use the autopilot for a more accurate approach and earlier recognition of deviation.	
PM Actions	Monitor flight path and speed. Call wind variations. Call vertical speed. When clear of shear report to ATC.			
Active	Config ≥ 1 3s after liftoff to 1300ft 1300ft to 50ft on landing	Active <2300 ft RA Alerts <100kt 50ft to 1500ft on climb out 1500ft to 50ft on landing		
Note	If windshear is detected by this system or by pilot observation the recovery procedure must be applied	If a positive verification that no hazard exists, then the alert may be disregarded as long as: - There are no signs of possible windshear conditions - The reactive windshear system is operational		

PFD Indications

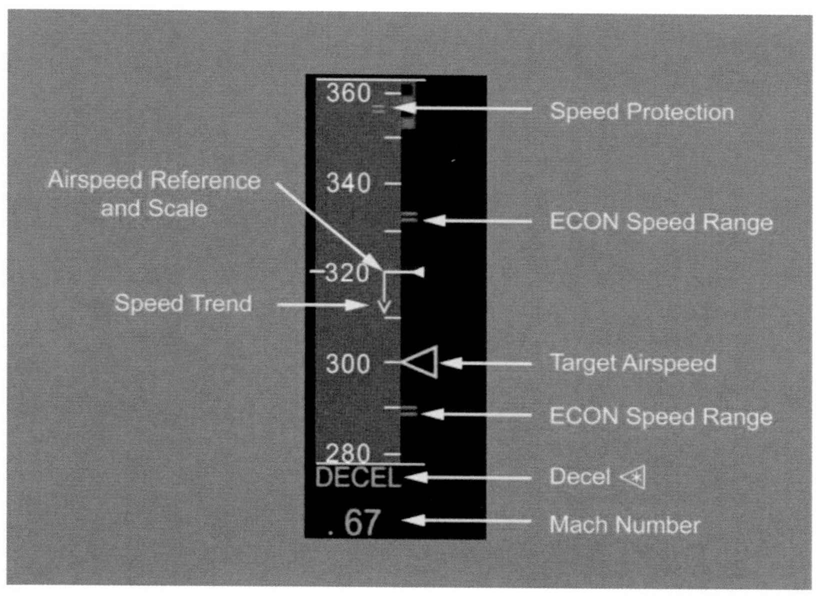

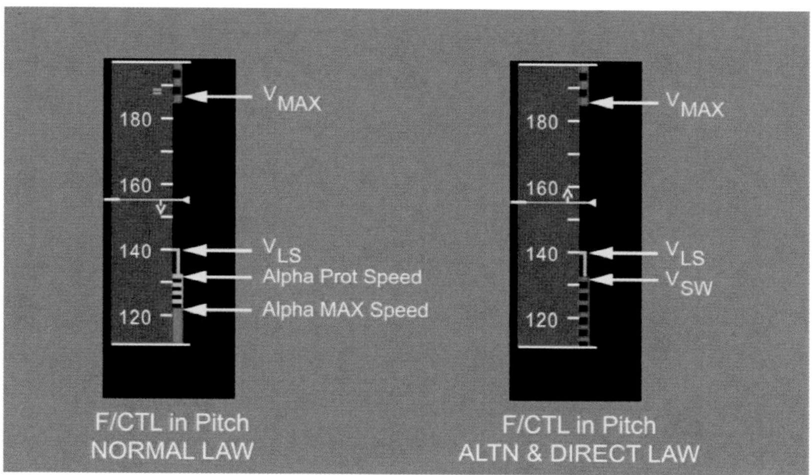

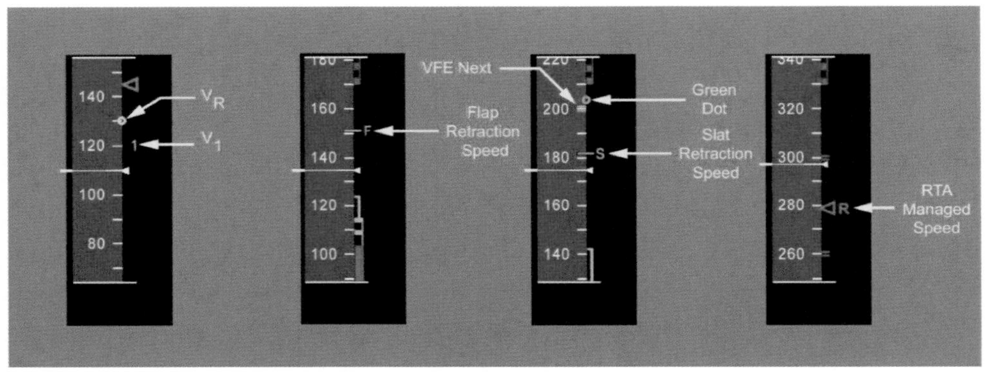

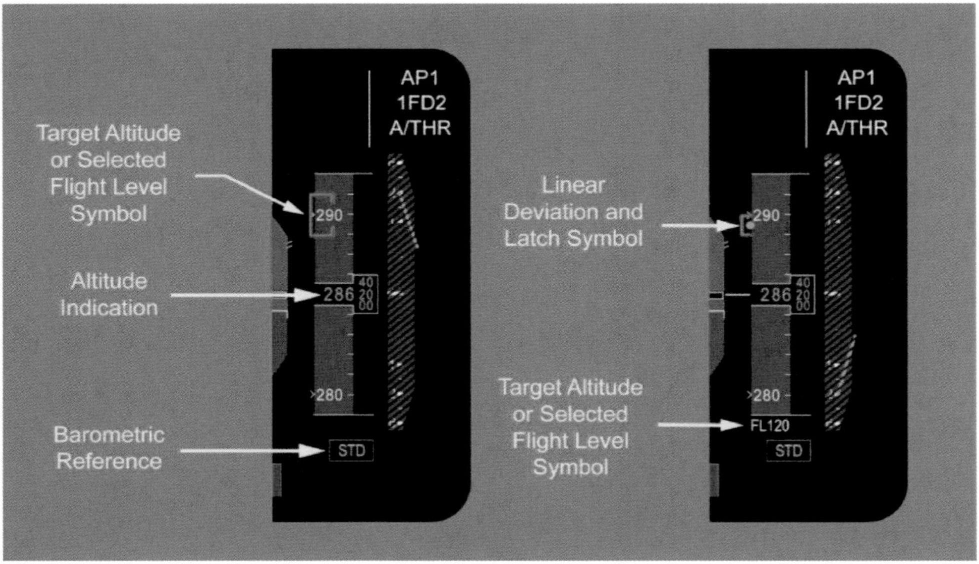

AP1
1FD2
A/THR

Target Altitude or Selected Flight Level Symbol

Altitude Indication

Barometric Reference

290
286
280
STD

AP1
1FD2
A/THR

Linear Deviation and Latch Symbol

Target Altitude or Selected Flight Level Symbol

290
286
280
FL120
STD

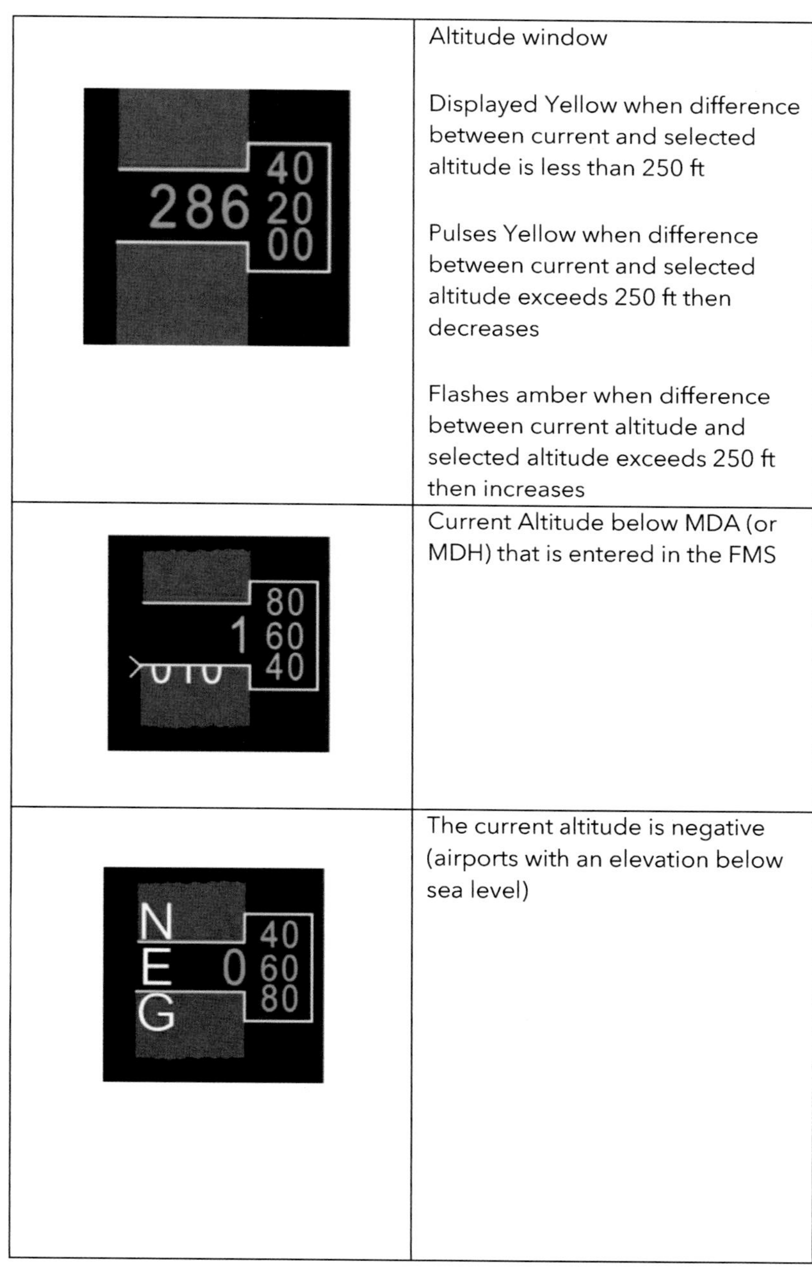

	Altitude window Displayed Yellow when difference between current and selected altitude is less than 250 ft Pulses Yellow when difference between current and selected altitude exceeds 250 ft then decreases Flashes amber when difference between current altitude and selected altitude exceeds 250 ft then increases
	Current Altitude below MDA (or MDH) that is entered in the FMS
	The current altitude is negative (airports with an elevation below sea level)

FL120	Altitude with Selected or Managed vertical guidance
290	The altitude target is within the altitude scale
FL120	Altitude constraint with managed vertical guidance outside of the altitude scale
290	An altitude constraint when the vertical guidance is managed. Within the altitude scale
FL060	Selected speed with vertical approach mode engaged *Disregards altitude target when approach mode engaged*
060	Selected altitude with vertical approach mode engaged *Disregards altitude target when approach mode engaged*

ND Indications

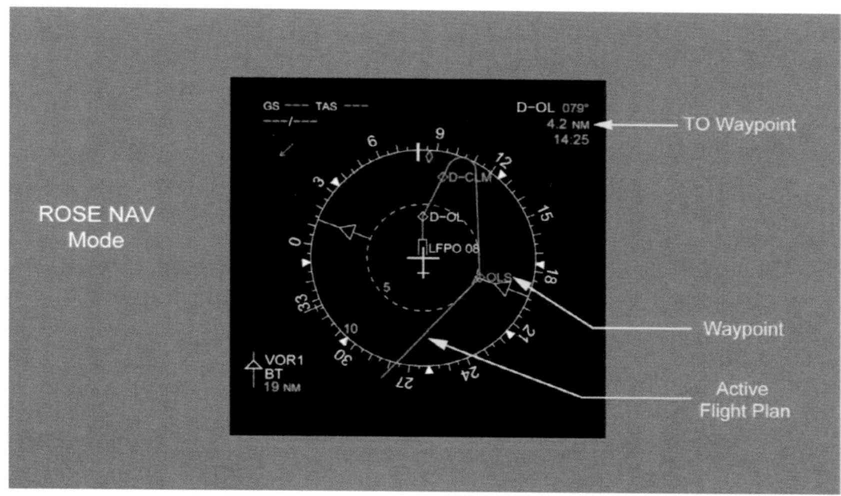

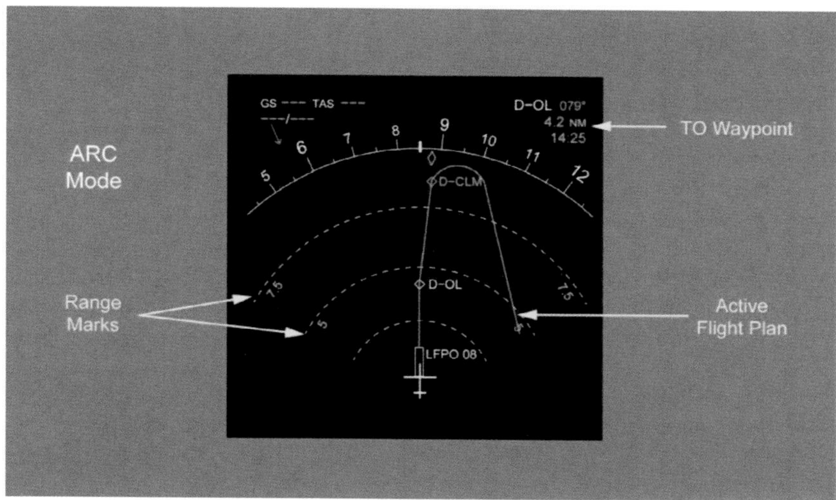

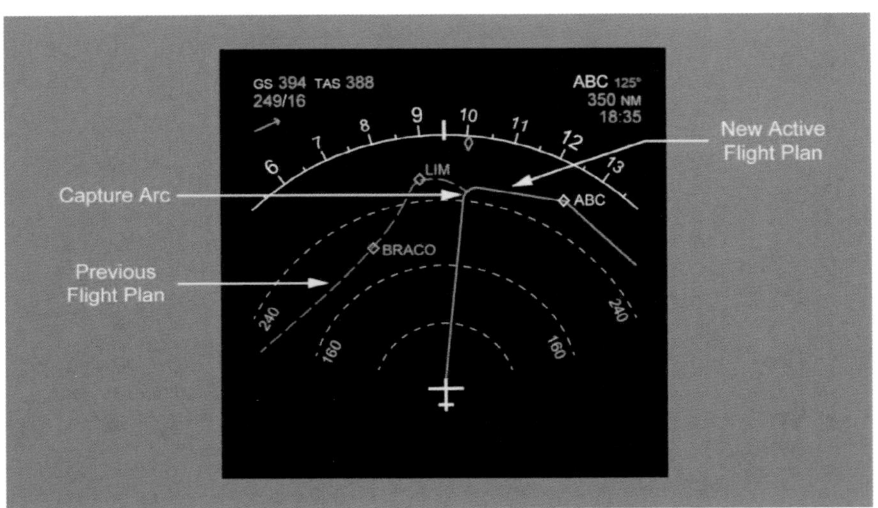
GS 394 TAS 388
249/16
ABC 125°
350 NM
18:35
6
7
8
9
10
11
12
13
LIM
ABC
BRACO
240
160
New Active
Flight Plan
Capture Arc
Previous
Flight Plan

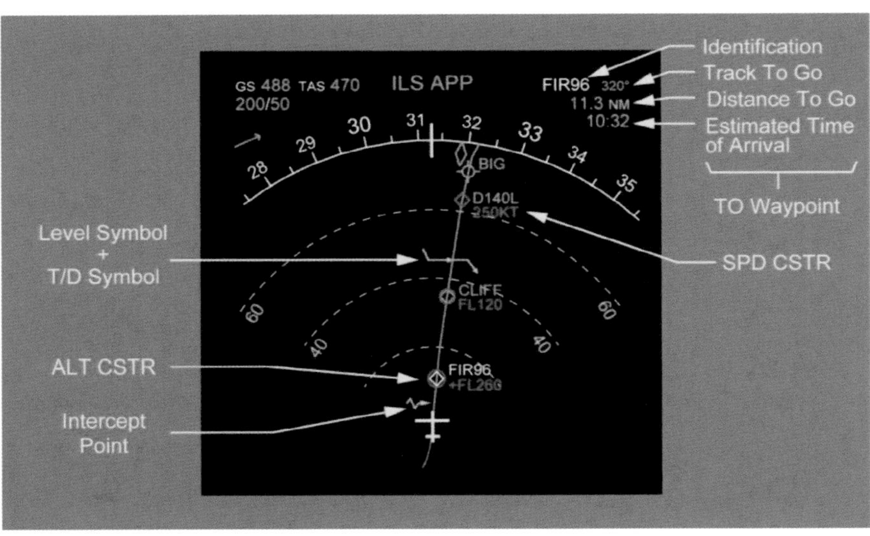
GS 488 TAS 470
200/50
ILS APP
FIR96 320°
11.3 NM
10:32
28
29
30
31
32
33
34
35
BIG
D140L
250KT
CLIFE
FL120
FIR96
+FL260
60
40
Identification
Track To Go
Distance To Go
Estimated Time
of Arrival
TO Waypoint
SPD CSTR
Level Symbol
+
T/D Symbol
ALT CSTR
Intercept
Point

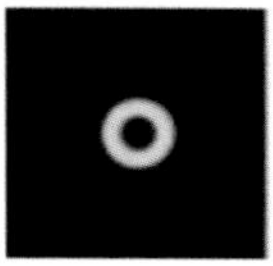	DME or TACAN
	VOR
	VOR / DME
	NDB
	ILS or LOC Approach Selected
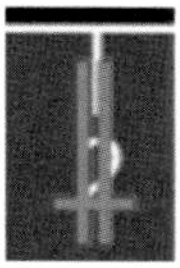	NPA Approach with FLS for lateral guidance is selected
OM	Aircraft over the Outer Marker
MM	Aircraft over the Middle Marker
IM	Aircraft over the Inner Marker

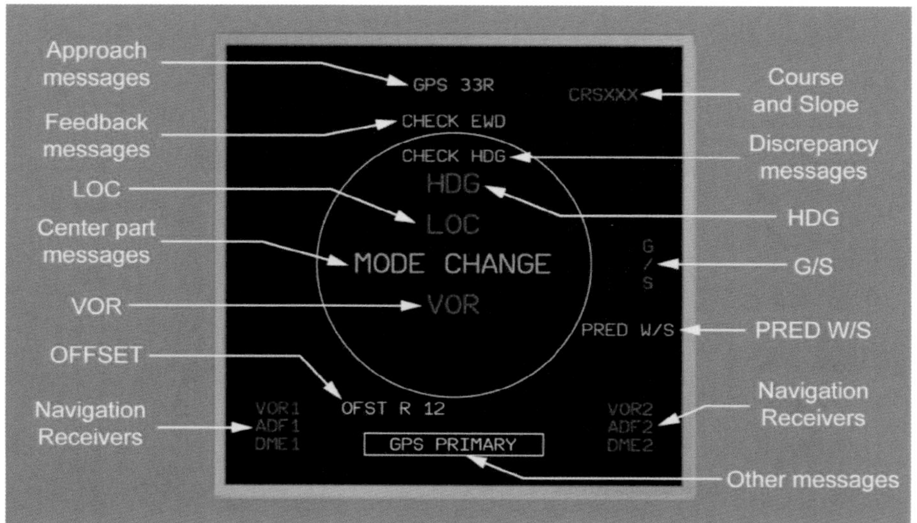
Approach messages
GPS 33R
CRSXXX
Course and Slope
Feedback messages
CHECK EWD
CHECK HDG
Discrepancy messages
HDG
LOC
LOC
HDG
Center part messages
MODE CHANGE
G / S
G/S
VOR
VOR
PRED W/S
PRED W/S
OFFSET
OFST R 12
Navigation Receivers
VOR1
ADF1
DME1
VOR2
ADF2
DME2
Navigation Receivers
GPS PRIMARY
Other messages

Flight Mode Annunciator (FMA) Modes

Autothrust Operation	Vertical Modes	Lateral Modes	Approach Capabilities	Auto Flight Status
TOGA	SRS	RWY	CAT 1	AP 1
FLX	ALT	RWY TRK	CAT 2	AP 2
MCT	ALT*	GA TRK	CAT 3 SINGLE	AP 1 + 2
CLB	ALT CRZ	TRACK	CAT 3 DUAL	1 FD 2
IDLE	ALT CST	HDG	DH XXX	1 FD
ASYM	V/S	NAV	MDA XXXX	FD 2
A. FLOOR	CLB	LOC		1 FD 1
TOGA LK	DES	LOC*		2 FD 2
THR LK	OP CLB	APP NAV		2 FD
MAN TOGA	EXP CLB			FD 1
MAN FLEX	EXP DES			A/THR
MAN MCT	G/S			
THR CLB	FINAL			
THR LVR	V/S +/- XXXX			
THR SPEED	FPA +/- XXXX			
THR IDLE				
SPEED				
MACH				
LVR CLB				
LVR MCT				
LVR ASYM				

COMBINED MODES
LAND
FLARE
ROLL OUT
FINAL APP

FMA MESSAGES
USE MAN PITCH TRIM
MAN PITCH TRIM ONLY
DECELERATE
MORE DRAG
VERTICAL DISCON AHEAD
CHECK APP SEL
SET GREEN DOT SPD
SET HOLD SPEED
MACH SEL .XX
SPEED SEL XXX

Auto Thrust Modes	
TOGA	Auto Thrust armed, thrust lever in TOGA detent
FLEX	Auto thrust armed. Represents Flex Temp set in MCDU T/O Perf page
MCT	Single Engine - Auto thrust armed with most forward thrust lever in MCT detent
CLB	Auto thrust armed with most forward thrust lever in CLB detent, aircraft has reached acceleration altitude
IDLE	Auto thrust armed with most forward thrust lever in CLB detent. Idle power commanded. Followed by low energy warning if engines remain at IDLE for a predetermined time
SPEED / MACH	Auto thrust armed. Thrust will vary as required to maintain vertical path commanded. Airspeed ignored if vertical path cannot be maintained.
ASYM	A/THR is armed but both thrust levers are not in the same detent
A.FLOOR	In Alpha Floor conditions, A/THR is engaged and TOGA commanded regardless of thrust lever position
TOGA LK	TOGA LK is engaged following Alpha Floor engagement. A/THR must be disconnected and re-armed again to regain A/THR control
THR LK	A/THR has been disconnected by the A/THR p/b on FCU or the A/THR has failed. Thrust is locked at the last known position until thrust levers are moved
MAN TOGA	Auto thrust is armed with most forward thrust lever in TOGA detent
MAN FLEX	Auto thrust armed with most forward thrust lever in FLX/MCT detent. Represents Flex Temp set in T/O Perf page on MCDU
MAN MCT	Auto thrust armed with most forward thrust lever in the FLX/MCT detent
MAN THR	2 Engines - Auto thrust armed, most forward thrust lever above CLB detent, but not in FLX/MCT or TOGA detent 1 Engine - Auto thrust armed, thrust lever above FLX/MCT but not in TOGA detent
THR MCT	Single Engine - Auto thrust armed, with most forward thrust lever in FLX/MCT detent. If other thrust lever is below FLX/MCT detent, thrust for that engine commanded by TLA. Will be accompanied by a LVR ASYM FMA message and AUTO FLT ECAM message

THR CLB	Auto thrust armed with forward most thrust lever in the CLB detent - Climb thrust commanded. If other thrust lever is below CLB detent, thrust for that engine commanded by TLA. Will be accompanied by a LVR ASYM FMA message and AUTO FLT ECAM message
THR LVR	Auto thrust armed with most forward thrust lever above the IDLE detent and below CLB detent. Thrust commanded by the TLA. Airspeed (Managed or Selected) will be maintained by varying pitch. Will be accompanied by a LVR CLB FMA message and a AUTO FLT ECAM message. (LVR MCT if single engine)
THR IDLE	Auto thrust armed with most forward thrust lever above the IDLE detent and anywhere up to and including the CLB detent. (MCT single engine) Airspeed (Managed or Selected) will be maintained by varying pitch
LVR CLB	Flashing white, during initial climb will occur at the thrust reduction altitude, programmed into the T/O PERF page on MCDU
LVR MCT	Flashing white - is used to prompt the crew to set the thrust levers to the MCT detent. During T/O it will illuminate if an engine is lost or for a single engine Go Around. In both cases it occurs at Green Dot but only if EO CLR was not selected on MCDU.
LVR ASYM	Indicates that A/THR is armed but both thrust levers are not in the same detent.

Vertical Modes	
SRS	Speed Reference System is engaged. Aircraft will fly the vertical path appropriate for the phase of flight T/O = V2 + 10 T/O (Eng Fail) = V2 Go Around = Vapp or current speed if higher Windshear = SRS will allow the speed to decrease to maintain 120 fpm climb SRS is only available when at least one FD is on and flap handle is greater than Flaps 1
ALT*	The FCU altitude has been captured. If a new altitude is selected prior to ALT engagement the FCU will revert to V/S until a new vertical mode is selected.
ALT	An FCU altitude which is not selected as the cruise altitude, has been engaged. Will be maintained as a hard altitude.
ALT CRZ	The FCU altitude which is the pre-programmed cruise altitude, has been engaged. Will be maintained as a soft altitude +/- 50 ft of the FCU altitude.
ALT CST*	Indicates a CLB or DES altitude constraint has been engaged and the FCU altitude is above (CLB) or below (DES) the constraint altitude.
CLB	Vertical Navigation is engaged, all constraints will be met (unless the FCU altitude is below the constraint altitude) Nav mode must be engaged. If NAV mode is lost or changed CLB will revert to OP CLB
DES	Vertical navigation is engaged, all constraints will be met. If NAV mode is lost or changed, DES will revert to OP DES. If DES is pushed prior to TOD, the aircraft will descend at around 900-1000 fpm. Once the profile is regained, it will use the ECON speed range of +/- 20 kts to maintain it. VNAV calculates an IDLE descent from TOD to the first constraint, then a straight line descent for the next segment. *If the aircraft levels off at an intermediate altitude, selecting PROG page and entering your altitude will force the VNAV to recalculate the descent. This will allow you to change speeds on the descent page.*

OP CLB	Climb utilizing the climb profile speeds at thrust climb will be flown. Aircraft will climb to FCU altitude and ignore altitude constraints. Will attempt to maintain the profile speed by varying pitch.
EXP CLB	A climb at green dot will be flown. Disengaged by selecting another vertical mode.
EXP DES	In idle descent at M 0.8 / 340 kts Disengaged by selecting another vertical mode.
G/S*	ILS Glideslope has been engaged. Once captured, the aircraft will ignore all FCU altitudes to maintain GS
FINAL	The vertical deviation path of an Approach Nav has been engaged. Using IR data, the FMGC will build its own vertical path. This is built from a point 50 ft over the approach end of the runway back to the final approach altitude. FINAL engages automatically when the aircraft intercepts this vertical path.
V/S +/- XXXX	A Selected vertical speed has been commanded. The aircraft will use pitch and thrust to maintain the selected V/S.
FPA +/- X.X	A selected flight path angle has been commanded. The aircraft will use pitch and thrust to maintain the selected FPA. *The FPA is relative to the aircraft and not a fixed point on the ground*

Lateral Modes	
RWY	Provides a steering command utilizing the localizer for the departure runway from takeoff through to 30 ft. A LOC must be associated with the runway in use. If the LOC signal is lost during the TO roll, a memorised track will be flown.
RWY TRK	Provides a lateral path along the extended runway centreline for all runways from 30 ft AGL, unless NAV mode is engaged.
GA TRK	Provides a lateral path based on the actual aircraft track at the time a GA was initiated.
HDG / TRK	The heading or track selected in the FCU window will be flown. If the HDG knob is pulled before it is turned, the aircraft will turn in the direction the knob is rotated. If the desired heading is set prior to pulling the knob, the aircraft will turn in the direction to make the shortest possible turn.
NAV	Lateral navigation is engaged to fly the flightplan in the MCDU. NAV in blue on line 2 indicates that NAV is armed. A cross check error should be present to indicate your displacement from the desired course. If not, then LNAV will not intercept the course you have selected.
APP NAV	The APPR pb has been pushed and the FMGC is flying the selected approach.
LOC	The LOC course is engaged. LOC* in blue for capture, LOC in blue on line 2 when armed. ILS pb need not be selected on for the AP to fly an ILS approach. Monitor raw data.

Combined Vertical / Lateral Modes	
LAND	At 400 ft AGL the dividing line on the FMA column 2 & 3 disappears along with G/S and LOC and a single mode common to both vertical and lateral guidance is engaged. LAND appears first to indicate that approach guidance can no longer be disengaged on the FCU. From this point on, the crew must select TOGA to activate the GA mode and disengage the APPR mode.
FLARE	At approximately 40 ft RA, LAND is replaced by FLARE (30 ft for an autoland)
ROLL OUT	Lateral guidance is provided for tracking the LOC along the runway
FINAL APP	The combined mode for a non ILS approach, FINAL is engaged for vertical NAV and APP NAV is engaged for vertical NAV, the APP pb has been pushed.

Approach Capability	
CAT 1	CAT 1 Approach may be flown (autoland not avail)
CAT 2	CAT 1 autoland approaches may be flown to CAT II/III runways
CAT 3 SINGLE	CAT II autoland approaches may be flown to CAT II/III runways. CAT 3 single will be annunciated until the second AP is coupled - (Fail Passive)
CAT 3 DUAL	CAT III autoland approaches may be flown to CAT III runways
MDA XXXX	Decision height for ILS approaches or MAP altitude for non precision approaches has been entered in the PERF page of the MCDU. At this altitude the altimeter will change to amber.
DH XXX	Radio altimeter for CAT II and CAT III approach has been entered in the PERF page of the MCDU